What thou wilt
Traditional and Innovative trends in Post-Gardnerian Witchcraft

What thou wilt
Traditional and Innovative trends in Post-Gardnerian Witchcraft

Jon Hanna

evertype

2010

Published by Evertype, Cnoc Sceichín, Leac an Anfa, Cathair na Mart, Co. Mhaigh Eo, Éire. *www.evertype.com*.

A catalogue record for this book is available from the British Library.

ISBN-10 1-904808-43-3
ISBN-13 978-1-904808-43-5

Typesetting by Michael Everson. Set in Baskerville and Excalibur SCF.

Cover design by Michael Everson. Photograph of the candle by Matthew Bowden, *www.digitallyrefreshing.com*. Photograph of the author by Al Higgins.

Printed and bound by LightningSource.

Contents

Dedication

To my mother
Marie Hanna *née* Doran
1948–2004

Foreword

It's a privilege to be asked to write a few words to introduce the work of a new author. When the author is one of my own students and initiates, it's even more than a privilege—it's an honour.

In the years I've been running a coven, I have always looked to my coven members and students to push their own boundaries, to look at, learn, and hopefully experience the wider picture of witchcraft and magic as well as those which are confined to our own tradition. In this light, one of the things they are required to do is to write an essay which explores some aspect of the Craft itself. Most often the contents of this essay will be something that covers an esoteric aspect of the Craft, such as the exploration of aspects of Deity or Magic, or it might explore the more practical aspects of Craft, such as spellcraft or herblore. So, when Jon wrote the outline for his Second Degree essay, as his teacher my first thought was "This is going to be interesting." This was because I thought that this is something that he would be well suited to write, because he had worked within a different structure of Wicca and it might well serve to highlight for him the differences he has encountered within the two forms of working, allowing him to process and integrate them. From my point of view, the integration of previous experience with current process is very important on every level—intellectually, psychologically, psychically, emotionally, and spiritually.

His explorations here are very different to other books that have attempted to look at the different strands of Wicca and Witchcraft. Unlike *Drawing Down the Moon*, by Margot Adler or *The Pagan Path* by Janet and Stewart Farrar, this is not a book that draws upon individual practices and draws conclusions, but rather, he takes an overview and looks at the different strands of Post-Gardnerian Wicca and Witchcraft from a much broader point of view, looking at the wider societal influences that have caused many of the changes within the various strains of Wicca and Witchcraft.

I particularly applaud his choice of terminology, by choosing the term "Innovative" over "Eclectic", Jon has managed to avoid using a term that is often thought of in emotive terms within the practice of Witchcraft and Wicca, often engendering feelings of inferiority or superiority and, occasionally, both. This has been something that has been a constantly recurring factor within the different strands of witchcraft since Gardner's time. I well remember coming across the feeling in the 80s and even the 90s, that the more innovative trends in witchcraft had to be defended in some way, mostly by the people who practised them. Jon does not defend or attack anything here, he presents things in a factual way, researching as thoroughly as he is able and then leaves us to draw our own conclusions with regard to the importance of the differences in working, view of working tools, Books of Shadows, training and the political, public and private faces of practice.

My second thought on reading Jon's outline was, "Hmmm, this is an ambitious project, how on earth is he going to keep it confined to 10,000 words?" Obviously, he didn't, and I didn't have the heart to tell him to cut it down to the required length, and I'm glad I didn't. Jon has written a work that not only is interesting, but I think will prove to be a resource book for all of those who are seeking their own paths.

Barbara Lee
High Priestess, Serpent Coven
Dublin, Samhain 2009

Preface

"He wrote the book." This most unfair expression suggests an apotheosis of expertise. What conviction one must need to publish! Certainly more than I would have possessed without the encouragement of others.

In the course of this work, I touch briefly upon the problem of self-efficacy—of accurately judging one's ability and achievements. While relevant here only in passing, it is not just a fascinating and sometimes amusing problem, but also one of importance to us all: How do we assess our own works' worth? Why do some believe themselves gifted in the face of evident failure, while some clearly talented people are racked with self-doubt, even as they are lauded? Most importantly, do not all of us both overestimate and underestimate our skills, as we move between different tasks?

Personally, I consider myself a fair writer while my fingers are upon a keyboard, and a poor one the moment I rest, to the extent that right now, I am inclined towards confidence in this preface and doubt in what follows.

It does not help that in the course of this book I mention so lucid a writer as Stewart Farrar. Nor that I mention Doreen Valiente, the great poetess of the Craft, who wears her laurels still, in the Summerlands. I mention polemicists like Dworkin whose words bleed compassion, scholars of great insight and erudition like Hutton and Heselton, and a great many popular writers who fired the imaginations of multitudes. And of course, I mention the founders of several Traditions of the Craft, including my own. Bringing such to the reader's mind, I put my writing in the company of the writings of those others—a truly daunting prospect. I am just a witch with a book, a very common creature these days.

Hence, I must offer great thanks to all those who have so-far complimented this work, starting with witches ranging in experience from seeker to elder, interested outsiders, and finally to Michael Everson, who reversed the conventional process in which it is the author that tries to persuade the publisher that a book should be brought out. I would not have allowed myself to see as much value in this work without their encouragement.

The value I now allow myself to see, is in two places.

The first is in my original goal of describing by difference. The earlier descriptions of most modern witchcraft naturally assume a Christian or post-Christian audience, with little or no previous knowledge of the Craft, and address what is remarkable to that perspective. That we honour the divine feminine, that we perform magic, that we have a non-Mosaic ethic, and that we work in small groups, were each remarkable to such an audience, as perhaps were some statements made to distance ourselves from the image of the accused devil-worshipper and the fairy-tale villainess. The value of this approach is obvious, but it is also limited. In assuming a reasonable knowledge of the Craft and drawing comparison not between it and the more widely-known religions, but between different forms of witchcraft now in existence, there is the opportunity to look at aspects of the Craft with a narrower focus. The insights on offer, to students of any form of witchcraft or to the interested outsider, in how we are different to each other, should differ from the now-familiar ways in which we are often compared to the largest religion in the West.

These insights should also, I hope, be different to some readers than they were to me. I own to my biases: I am an Alexandrian initiate with a great love for that Tradition, and though my writing here is informed by also working other forms of witch-craft, it is only from that position as an Alexandrian that I can speak. Yet if I have had even middling success in objectively, then there will be cases of my describing how innovations differ from the traditions we keep to, where those who have a similar love for those innovations will feel they have the advantage in the comparison. I like to imagine that a reader from outside of the New Forest-descended Traditions will, at least once, find it puzzling that I seem to them to be describing their practice more favourably than my own.

At the very least, I would hope that if I nowhere achieve such a balance as to allow this, that they will feel I have given them their due.

The differences within modern witchcraft—not just across the line between Innovative and Traditional, but within each of them, and between them and those that owe little to Gardner—often tend to be expressed in terms of polarization, disdain, and rumour. Within modern Paganism we often commend ourselves for our tolerance, and it would be nice to believe that our peaceful record doesn't lie solely in our lack of the army or navy needed to commit atrocities. Yet this oft-vaunted tolerance is not always in evidence. At the same time, to seek it in a self-imposed silence, to "just get along", is no solution either. What it leaves unsaid, it leaves unfinished. It can only postpone disagreements, not clarify them.

It seems clear to me, when I have witnessed such disagreements, that parties are often talking at cross-purposes to an extent often unclear to at least one of them. We have enough differences within modern witchcraft to harbour very different views, but we are close enough neighbours to use very similar language, albeit often in sharply differing ways. The effect is to lead to false senses of consensus, and misunderstandings of the other's position, that makes each other's perspectives seem less reasonable than they are. Such misunderstanding of another's meaning is beloved of the writers of situational comedy, but considerably less enjoyable anywhere else. For example, I explain in the course of this work why much that is new in witchcraft seems to me more dogmatic than Traditional Wicca, yet that Traditional Wicca is often seen as the more dogmatic is a widely-attested viewpoint. Since witches of both forms value their lack of dogma—to the extent that the term *dogma* becomes invective—it is not fruitful to simply refer to each other as such. Nor is it fruitful to think of each other as such, but not say it, or worse still, to say it only in private. The only prospect for a tolerant view of each other is to understand the differing perspectives that lead to this difference. We must seek not to always agree, but to understand the nature of our disagreements. If this volume can help this, then that is the second place I see value in it.

And maybe elsewhere too. I am a young witch, and as such, inclined to look at my future in the Craft as stretching ahead for quite some distance. Hopefully, some way along this path, taking another look at what I present here, I will not find too much embarrassment, and will myself take from it some fresh insight or value, that my younger self has placed in these sentences unbeknownst to me now.

I must give considerable thanks to Barbara Lee and Gavin Morrison, for many reasons, but especially for asking a student to write an essay, and not getting too annoyed when enthusiasm for his subject led to him presenting something much longer than anticipated.

Among other examples of their hospitality, Radella Corbin's coven took me on a fruitful shopping trip that allowed me to acquire some research material at low Canadian prices. (Or maybe I just spend money more freely when not my own currency.) Radella was later to provide many useful comments on an earlier draft of this work, of which making me aware of the work of Lugones and Rosezelle stands out as particularly strengthening one section. Any remaining weaknesses, there or elsewhere, are of course my own.

As indeed are all opinions expressed, and those acknowledged here may not agree with them.

Finally, my beloved Joanna must be thanked for many things, particularly for her patience when I would say, "Just a minute, when I'm finished this bit," and she knew better than I, that I would take considerably longer.

Jon Hanna
Dublin, Samhain 2009

Chapter One

On Wicca and Wicca

"You keep using that word. I do not think it means, what you
think it means."

—William Goldman, *The Princess Bride*.

"What's in a name? That which we call a rose
By any other name would smell as sweet;"
—William Shakespeare, "Romeo and Juliet," Act II, scene ii.

1.1 What's in a Name?

The oft-debated history of the emergence of Wicca into the
public eye, following the publication of Gerald Gardner's non-
fiction works on the subject [Gardner 1954 & Gardner 1959], and
the later influence of Alex Sanders and others upon that
movement, has been much written about, and has been the focus
of much recent research.[1] The ongoing disagreements on the
precise relationship of Gardner, Sanders and other figures of the
time to the traditions of the Wicca, and to what went before them
(what we might call Wiccan prehistory) is not relevant to this
work. What suffices, is that by the early 1960s there was an

---

1   For example, Heselton 2000, Hutton 1999, Heselton 2003, and
    Hutton 2003 between them reflect two positions in an ongoing debate on
    just what can be justifiably said on the matter by historians.

appreciable degree of public knowledge of the Wicca, which has continued to grow since.

More important to this work is the question of what exactly Wicca is. At the time of writing, common definitions are:

- The priesthood of a collection of related mystery-tradition fertility cults, practising cross-gender initiation and witch-craft, holding a shared initiatory lineage to certain covens in the New Forest region of England.
- Any form of witchcraft (that is to say, a synonym).
- Modern Pagan witchcraft.
- Forms of Pagan witchcraft and/or religion including: those of the New Forest lineages, those of the New Forest lineages but which do not continue the traditional practices, and others which have been heavily influenced by what is publicly stated by or about members of the New Forest lineages.

There are also some rougher definitions that are used in practice, though they tend towards imprecision, with people perhaps using it for any form of witchcraft tied to a religious view, any form other than Satanic witchcraft (generally because the speaker frowns upon Satanism), and other even vaguer distinctions based on whichever aspects the speaker sees as particularly Wiccan, perhaps even excluding those Wiccans close in practice to Gardner, Sanders, the Mohs, etc.

These latter definitions are hardly definitions at all, and the very difficulty with such definitions recurs repeatedly in works on Wicca and modern witchcraft, as demonstrated by attempts at a firmer definition relying heavily on imprecise terms, and making no stronger statements than "most" or "practically all". [NWC 2004].

This work focusses on the first and fourth definition, and the relationship between the two movements so described. Since all such witchcraft owes something to the influence of Gardner's publications and activities, albeit in different ways, I refer to such witchcraft as a whole as *Post-Gardnerian Witchcraft*[2].

In this work, *Traditional Wicca* will be used to refer to the first; those which continue the lineages and practices. While the term *British Traditional Wicca* has been suggested by the New Wiccan Church as a more specific term [NWC 2004], which is gaining currency, this term is not presently widespread outside of the US and Canada, and raises its own difficulties.[3] It is as a compromise between the advantages of that term and concision, that I use the term *Traditional Wicca*. For reasons that will be given below, the term *Innovative Witchcraft* will be used for those forms of Post-Gardnerian witchcraft which are not Traditional Wicca.

These very definitions would entail that Traditional Wicca preceded Innovative Witchcraft (if we dismiss testimony from a few groups that claim a long lineage and that Gardner borrowed wholesale from them, increasingly a position only of the most marginal traditions—for example Anonymous 2004), and implies a relationship in which the cultural and technological borrowings are entirely in one direction. This is often accepted by

---

2   Clearly then, I mean *Post-Gardnerian* as in "after Gardner" rather than "after the Gardnerian Tradition". Hence Gardnerians are also Post-Gardnerian in this sense.

3   For example, the editor's notes for page on "British Traditional Wicca" [Wikipedia 2006]. Here an attempt to define "British Traditional Wicca" for an encyclopaedic entry raises an objection from someone who understands the similar (and identical when initialized) term "British Traditional Witchcraft" as referring to non-Wiccan traditions native to Britain.

practitioners of both, though obviously with differing opinions on the value of this split.

As we look closer, this becomes less clear. To begin with, it is not entirely clear from Gardner's writings just what the relationship between witches generally and those he refers to as *The Wica* is.

To a modern Traditional Wiccan reader today, it certainly seems that The Wica, the most common spelling in current usage, are those particular witches with which Gardner was personally familiar, and who accepted him as one of their own. This reading, however, hinges on turns of phrase rather than any explicit statement, so those who would claim *The Wica* as a term within witchcraft for all witches will point to exactly the same passages to make their counter-arguments.

A related complication is that, at that time, Traditional Wiccans often wouldn't have accepted many practitioners of other forms of witchcraft, including Innovative Witchcraft, as witches at all. In particular, the self-initiated, or those of a lineage which ultimately derives from a self-initiate, would not be accepted as witches as, "only a witch can make a witch". With knowledge of the older non-Wiccan forms of witchcraft being limited due to a great lack of communication compared to today, *Wicca* was indeed seen as synonymous with *witch*, for the simple reason that only Traditional Wiccans—to apply the term retroactively—were seen as witches at all. Stewart Farrar not only described *Wicca* as an internal term witches use for their religion, in his first book on the subject, but admitted that he knew nothing about the lines now labelled *Traditional Initiatory Witchcraft*, save that they work robed [Farrar 1971]. Such an admission would not be seen in a book on witchcraft today. This is partly because not

4

every author would be as honest as Farrar in ever admitting igno-rance on any matter—even when they should be! Partly also, Farrar was new to the Craft, being initiated in the course of his writing that book, and not at that time claiming expertise, but rather to be writing as a reporter. Mainly though, the availability, if not always the quality, of information obtainable by even the most cursory inquiries today is vastly beyond what was available to the most devoted of seekers at the time, until they managed to make personal contact with someone of a particular form of the Craft.

That many Traditional Wiccans maintain a claim to the term as explicitly referring to themselves alone, now that they will recognize others' claims to being witches, seems likely to at least in part have been by comparison with avowedly non-Wiccan lines, such as those of Feri, the various lines claiming descent from Robert Cochrane, and those who claim a family tradition. Were the only people claiming to be witches the Traditional Wiccans on the one hand, and the self-initiates on the other, then perhaps if the times had still changed in such a way that many Traditionals were more inclined to recognize some outside of their own lines as witches, they would also have ceded the word *wicca* to them. However, this same increase in acceptance of those outside of Traditional Wicca came alongside a greater knowl-edge, such practices as those mentioned above, and non-English speaking lines like Stregaria (an Italian tradition). Indeed, such increased knowledge of those lines would in itself have led to their no longer thinking of themselves as the only witches in the world. As such, the reassessment that acknowledged witches outside of New Forest–descended lines would necessitate a reassessment of just what *Wicca* meant, to reflect the fact that other witches do not

5

use the word. To many Traditional Wiccans, the most obvious answer to that reassessment would be that The Wicca were those people they had always known as such. Those using the name without New Forest lineage and practice were seen as no more Wiccan after this more tolerant reassessment than they were before.

The counter-argument from those of Innovative Witchcraft is that *wicca* is the same as the Anglo-Saxon *wicċa*[4] and hence simply *is* the word for witch. This is probably true,[5] but even so we do not speak Anglo-Saxon! If the word *computer* can change so much in less than a century that it now only refers to electronic machines, and the people who once had *computer* as their job-description are largely forgotten, then surely *wicca* could have

---

4   The use of diacritical dots on *c*'s in Anglo-Saxon words to indicate the /tʃ/ sound now normally represented with the spelling *ch* is a modern convention, not an original feature of the language. It has the serendipitous advantage of resulting in the Anglo-Saxon *wicċa* being distinguished in spelling from the Modern English *wicca*, and I use the convention purely for this convenience.

5   It is just about plausible that the word is some sort of independent coinage that, while probably cognate with the Modern English *witch* and the Anglo-Saxon *wicċa*, is not the same as either. The one argument in favour of this suggestion is that Gardner describes the word as one he heard, not read, and *wicċa* is pronounced /'witʃːɑ/, not /wɪkə/ as the modern *wicca* is.

If we accept Gardner's claim that it is not his own coinage, it remains considerably more likely that the Anglo-Saxon word was adopted from a textual source and then pronounced as if it were modern English, perhaps influenced by Skeats' *Etymology* being quoted in (Leland 1891), a work that would have obvious interest to a witch. If this was the source, then the earliest the New Forest Coven or an ancestor coven could have adopted the term is 1891, though other sources for the word have been in existence for the entire history of the English language, so *wicca* could have been adopted from *wicċa* before that date.

changed to mean only some witches over the course of a millennium. Indeed, *wicca* is not actually used to mean *witch* in either usage.

Yet, precisely the same logic gives those in Innovative Witchcraft that wish to use the word, the final argument that words change, and the word is now used as they use it, at least as one sense among others.

1.2 Drawing Lines

There can be a difficulty in determining just which stream a practitioner belongs to or a text describes. While people who have lineage and training clearly descended from a Traditional Wiccan Tradition and maintain it as their sole practice are definitely Traditional Wiccans, and autodidactic self-initiates are clearly Innovative Witches, not everything is as clear-cut.

Traditional Wiccan method has always been capable of making use of techniques, views, and wordings from elsewhere. While the insistence upon core traditions makes it less fluid in this regard than Innovative Witchcraft, there is no reason why material developed by Innovative Witches would not find its way into the practices of a group of Traditional Wiccans, though it may not be considered "core".

More problematic still for an attempt at analysis, is the large number of people who engage in both Traditional and Innovative practice, or which have done one or the other at different points in their lives. Since this includes some of the writers who have had the greatest influence within both trends, this can be particularly important.

Additionally, the very borrowing of views and techniques from Traditional Wicca into Innovative Witchcraft, combined with the fact that most Innovative Witches are starting from a *tabla rasa* when they come to construct their practice, means that a Traditional Wiccan expressing a personal opinion as a Traditional Wiccan may have a stronger influence upon Innovative Witchcraft than upon Traditional Wicca, while quite definitely remaining Traditional in his or her own practice. As such, though the author may be a Traditional Wiccan, the influence will be largely upon the other stream under consideration. Defining any such artefact as firmly belonging to one stream or the other becomes close to impossible, and comparison with other sources must be a guide. It is also important to pay attention to the voice used at different parts of the same text; in particular to whether an author is currently describing the tradition they were passed, or their personal opinions about aspects of it.

Further, the sympathies of many Traditional Wiccan authors, particularly those with the most influence upon Innovative Witchcraft, may be more firmly with that stream than with Traditional Wicca when it comes to dissemination of information—after all, they may cover matters in books that Traditional Wiccans are going to learn during coven training anyway, and so it is the Innovative Witches that are the audience. Worse still for an analysis of this sort, their sympathies may change over time; Raymond Buckland, for example, is notable as both a defender and attacker of self-initiation at different times of his life. Indeed, an author's sympathies are unlikely to be polarized in a simplistic manner, but rather a perfectly human complex of different views on different topics.

Deeper problems come from the implied assumption that Traditional Wiccan practice has been essentially static, while all deviations can be viewed as innovation. It is certainly true that

Traditional Wicca represents a more narrowly defined range of practices, but it is not immune to history. One oft-referenced point is the attitude to homosexuality that Gardner exhibited and many repeated, which has been largely removed by the progress made by the Gay Rights Movement in changing the attitudes of Western society generally and of counter-cultures in particular. Even more notable is the relative promiscuity of initiations of both Gardner and Sanders [Hutton 1999, Guerra 2008, Farrar & Farrar 1984/Farrar & Farrar 1996], and of the first generation of their initiates, compared to the speed with which elevations would now be performed. Traditional Wiccan elders are now generally more cautious in this regard, while Innovative Witch-craft will contain many who will repeat the speed of elevation found in the early public history of Traditional Wicca, as well as containing some who start identifying themselves as Wiccan pretty much immediately upon learning about it.[6]

Another difficulty, is that with *Wicca* entering into the popular lexicon, it could be adopted by people with a lineage outside of Post-Gardnerian Witchcraft, who are hence outside of our scope of consideration, but without clear indication that this is so. Forms of witchcraft other than Traditional Wicca have always been with us. The boundaries and definitions quickly become matters of opinion, and as such whether a seventeenth-century

---

6　This could be argued to be a lesson that keeps being learned by new groups. Those with a Traditional training have the advantage of learning about the issues raised from their teachers, while Innovative Witches repeat the mistake. More reasonably though, one could argue that there are benefits to such speedy initiation which are more pronounced when a tradition has fewer members than when it has grown, and hence new groups repeat conditions also experienced by Gardner and Sanders, in which the benefits of such rapid progress outweigh the problems.

cunningman, an otherwise devout Christian who uses folk magic, a magic worker who is outside of any other defined tradition or ceremonial method, and so on, is or is not a witch, is in each case open to interpretation. Since *wicca* is sometimes treated as a perfect synonym of *witchcraft*, these other forms of witchcraft are sometimes also labelled *wicca*, sometimes against the protests of the practitioners, but often by the practitioners themselves. If we are to consider this retroactive labelling, there is a danger of opening the scope to the point of meaninglessness.

Finally, by 1974 there was also the emergence of Seax-Wica, [Buckland 1974] which makes use of the same word, but since it looks to Saxon culture, it is natural for it to adopt the Anglo-Saxon word *wicca* as a sort of "independent reclamation".[7] The separate use of the word, justified differently to that within Traditional Wicca, would probably have helped to diffuse and widen its use generally.

Well before this time though, we had several influences affecting the use of the word.

The first is the mismatch between the number of people made aware of Wicca by public personalities (such as Gardner, the Sanderses, the Bucklands, and the Farrars) and the number of people who could train would-be initiates, or at least refuse them training in such a way as to reduce the risk that they would, as Aidan Kelly puts it, "start an imitation based on Rosemary's Baby if they weren't let in" [Kelly 1994]. Hence, despite a rate of initiation and elevation that would be remarkable today, there were still disappointed seekers who had a sense of what they wanted, but were left to their own devices.

---

7   Though perhaps *Sax Wiccecræft* would have been a more accurate name for a Saxon-based witchcraft?

A second is the distribution of the *Pagan Way* material, intended to relieve this difficulty, much of which was clearly Wiccan-derived, and yet clearly also not subject to the same restrictions on transmission.

A third was the publication of Lady Sheba's *The Book of Shadows* [Sheba 1971], which makes use of the word *Wiccan* and contains several passages generally attributed to Doreen Valiente or otherwise claimed as belonging to Traditional Wicca.[8]

Each of these factors led to there being people outside of Traditional Wicca, but being influenced by it in practice to a greater or lesser extent.

The introduction of the concept of *Self-initiation*, examined in more detail later, had a strong effect upon the degree to which those working such forms of witchcraft could work independently of any previously existing group or tradition. At this point the split was complete. There were now two different groups, who were calling themselves *Wicca*, who need not have any contact with, and increasingly not even much awareness of, each other.

The split made, further severance was inevitable, due to something that long existed within Wicca, and indeed all forms of witchcraft: the practical willingness to make use of just about anything that works.

This has been noted already, in terms of the difficulty in precisely determining whether particular people are Traditional or not, without strong knowledge of their practice. Obviously, it leads to a great deal of variety within Traditional Wicca, but is balanced by traditions providing a framework with which to attach any such innovations and borrowings.

---

8   Compare with material described as such in Farrar & Farrar 1984.

Without the insistence upon tradition, and indeed with some aspects of the traditions remaining out of reach, the new strains of Wicca-inspired witchcraft naturally came to value borrowings and innovations more highly still. From the perspective of Traditional Wicca the result is a very eclectic mix indeed.

If anything is typical of these strains of witchcraft, it is this high value placed on innovation, whether continual or in the formation of a body of lore that would then crystallize into something that could be passed on as a new tradition. While Traditional Wiccans often label such strains *Eclectic witchcraft*, there are several problems with this term. The first is that from another perspective, one might label Traditional Wicca *eclectic*. What else would an outsider label traditions in whose liturgy one can find material originating with Kipling, Shakespeare, Leland, Crowley, Freemasonry and *The Carmina Gadelica* [Farrar & Farrar 1984], if only in turns of phrase, or which for public god names pair the Gaulish Cernunnos with the Tuscan Aradia?[9]

The second problem is that within these strains, *eclectic* is used to refer to people who deliberately take cultural and magical influences from a very wide range of sources, in a highly syncretistic manner. Non-traditional witches who concentrate upon a particular pantheon would often not consider themselves eclectic, but rather as Celtic, Germanic, Norse, Egyptian, Hellenic, or whatever other culture or material they most closely identified themselves with. Often this would be the case, even if some of their gap-filling was quite definitely eclectic by any stretch of the word—they would view this more as an eclectic

---

9   For that matter the Mohs used the term *American Eclectic Wicca*, to describe their practice prior to *eclectic* becoming more strongly connected with those who were outside of Traditional Wicca.

borrowing into an otherwise non-eclectic practice; or as being eclectic with a small "e", where deliberately more varied borrowings would be *Eclectic* with a capital "E".

Finally, the term could reasonably be applied to forms of witchcraft which have not borrowed anything from Traditional Wicca, do not self-describe as *Wicca*, and have had little impact upon the history of either of the strains examined here, nor the public view of them, and as such are not of interest to this work.

To avoid this difficulty, I am using the term *Innovative Witchcraft* for these strains of witchcraft. It has the advantage of being a generally positive term, while at the same time it does not entail an insult to Traditional Wicca by implying that the Traditional Wicca are not innovative; I feel that Traditional Wiccans would generally agree that while they value innovation, they do not value it over their traditions, and hopefully therefore none will take offence if I cede that word to other strains of witchcraft.

The term *Innovative Witchcraft* has the difficulty of not using the term *Wicca*, and as such appears to take sides in the debate on whether the term *Wiccan* applies to them or not. *Innovative Wicca*, though, while not just raising objections from the other side of that debate, could also raise objections from those Innovative Witches who agree that the word *Wicca* does not apply to them—while almost everyone who claims the term *Wiccan* also claims the term *witch*.[10] While part of the concept of this work is to examine

10 There are some exceptions; Silverlotus 2004 for example claims, "I am Wiccan, but I am not a Witch." Such people would appear to be devotees of some form of Neopagan religion which is faith-based rather than practice-based, and which includes little or no practice of magic, though it often would include a belief in the efficacy of magic, and a tolerant view of those who do use it. While they also represent a Post-Gardnerian stream of philosophy, they are by definition outside of the scope of the current work.

two groups which both use the name *Wicca*, some groups who do not use that word share much the same history.[11]

Innovative Witchcraft could be applied to a form of witchcraft that was developed from pure inspiration, or was influenced by non-New Forest traditions like Feri, in much the same way that those examined here were influenced by Traditional Wicca. While a possible difficulty with the term as a general coinage, such forms of witchcraft being beyond the scope of this work removes the difficulty here, if nowhere else.

This scope excludes a variety of religious and magical practice whose origins are outside of anglophone culture, including many where the aptness of the label *witchcraft* is debated. It also excludes Feri, The Regency, their descendants, and other modern forms of witchcraft which have a lineage dating back long enough to either pre-date Gardner, or at least date early enough to avoid the influence of the large amount of post-Gardnerian material now in circulation, without having to be deliberate in such exclusions.

Where people have been influenced by both Wicca and other forms of witchcraft, determining whether to consider them in scope or not is, by necessity, somewhat arbitrary. With the Roebuck Tradition, for example, while the Finnins received training from Ed Fitch and initiation from the Mohs, their primary identifiable influence was from the Clan of Tubal Cain [Finnin 2008], and so I deemed that tradition to be outside of my scope. On the other hand, much the same could be said about Starhawk and her Reclaiming tradition, with Feri being a greater direct influence than Wicca [Starhawk 1979]. Ultimately, the influence that Starhawk had on others who were also strongly

---

11 There may even be a difference of opinion within the same tradition, or even the same coven, on whether the term applies.

influenced by Wiccan sources, or who identify as Wiccan, was such that I could not ignore her.

A consolation is that in attempting to not just examine those works that have gained the largest degree of fame or notoriety, but also to at least touch the surface of the large number of publications, including the vast number of web publications, that come especially from the Innovative streams of witchcraft, it is inevitable that I will exclude a large amount of informative material, no matter how I define the scope.

Where terms like *Wicca* and *witchcraft* appear in italics in this work, as they do frequently above, I am considering them as terms, and examining them as signifiers rather than what they signify. Where I use the term *Wicca* unqualified by the adjective *Traditional* I am deliberately leaving the definition vague, and using it in a way which holds whether or not one includes any or all Innovative Witchcraft in that. At no point do I attempt to define the terms *witch* or *witchcraft*, except in so far that it is taken to include all Traditional Wicca and practically all Innovative Witchcraft. Debates on whether some practitioners of Innovative Witchcraft should be considered so far removed from Traditional Wicca, as to not be witches at all, and to just what further practices outside of any Post-Gardnerian influence should be considered witchcraft, I have also deemed out of scope.

Chapter Two

Traditions in the Craft
and Traditions of the Craft

"Because of our tradition, everyone knows who he is, and what
God expects him to do"
>   —Joseph Stein, "Fiddler on the Roof"

2.1 Denominations

At first blush, the word *tradition* is a straightforward one. *The Compact Oxford Dictionary* offers the definitions.

1. The transmission of customs or beliefs from generation to generation.
2. A long-established custom or belief passed on in this way.
3. An artistic or literary method or style established by an artist, writer, or movement, and subsequently followed by others. [OED 2005]

Each of these can be seen as directly applicable to Traditional Wiccan traditions. Customs and practices are passed from elders to new initiates (beliefs are a slightly different matter, though there is still an element of this happening), and these customs are considered their traditions. The third definition can be extended as applicable; some distinctions between Traditional Wicca and other religious or magical practices could be considered mainly a matter of style. Certainly some things will be identified as "feeling" Wiccan or non-Wiccan more immediately than one could reason about whether they belong in the Craft.

It is therefore completely within the common dictionary definitions of the word by which we say; *Gardnerian Tradition, Alexandrian Tradition, Mohsian Tradition,* and so on.

However, in doing so, we have hit upon another use of the term, by which people will use it to refer to religions or denominations within a particular religion. This usage is relatively rare compared to alternatives, such as *religion, denomination, creed,* etc., and normally only used when one is concerned with a cultural, religio-political or religio-historical context, rather than purely religious and spiritual differences. When Irish politicians talk of, "both traditions on this island",[12] they are using a phrase has has passed from cliché into idiom, and is immediately understood as referring not just to the Catholic and Protestant denominations, nor just to the Nationalist and Unionist political aspirations, but to the complex, often shifting way in which those religious, political, and other cultural perspectives interact. Here again, there is something particularly apt in Wiccan preference for this term over the term *denomination*—they see themselves as bound to their brethren not just through common religious expression, but as sharing a kinship that goes beyond that.

Still, it remains that the Traditional Wiccan Traditions are *traditions* in the dictionary senses of the word. This is not necessarily so with Innovative Witchcraft. Here a "Tradition" may be extremely new, having been consciously started rather than arrived at; may not yet actually have been passed on to anyone; and may very often die out before it ever is.

---

12 For example, President Mary McAleese, speaking at a commemoration of the Battle of Kinsale, 22 September 2001.

There are degrees of concious effort here. Ed Fitch's *Grimoire of Shadows* is hailed in the promotional material on the back cover of the 2002 edition as, "The Book That Launched a Thousand Traditions" [Fitch 2002], though in the preface he describes his surprise when a friend of a friend, Joe Lukach, referred to it as a tradition:

> "Ed," he said, "what you've written is a full tradition in itself. Didn't you realize that?"

Still, this creation was more a matter of serendipitous results, than a concious attempt to create a tradition. It may also be that Lukach means that he has written enough material that it *could* form a tradition, rather than it being fully a tradition as either of them would understand it.

Lukach was not a witch, but worked one of the Caribbean traditions. This brings us to another sense of the word *tradition*, that of a trend in magical practice which may or may not overlap with religious practice. It is probably this sense that Lukach was primarily considering, when he commented. Again, Traditional Wicca, and specific Traditional Wiccan Traditions, fit this sense of *tradition* also.

In this sense, there is still a strong implication of passed-down knowledge. However, for the most part people do not create *traditions*, they create *orders*. While orders such as the A∴A∴, the OTO or the Hermetic Order of the Golden Dawn, might be referred to as traditions, they were founded as orders, which then developed traditions, or worked with traditions that were (at least claimed as) pre-existing. Traditions did not spring full-formed like

18

Athena from the foreheads of Crowley and MacGregor Mathers, nor of Gardner and Sanders.

Contrasted to this is the publication of books which attempt to start "traditions" by describing them.

The closest approximation to the deliberate creation of a tradition that we can find in twentieth century Western esoterica outside of Wicca, is probably the publication of *Liber AL vel Legis*, with the entailed creation of a new stream of religious philosophy, and hence if the philosophy found adherents, as it did, a new tradition. What is notable here, is the degree of novelty held to be in the work. As such *Liber AL vel Legis* stands not so much in the company of the founding of new magical or religious orders, as it does with other revealed texts such as *al-Qur'ān*, or *The Book of Mormon*, ground-breaking works of religious philosophy such as Luther's *Theses*, or even with declarations of non-religious beliefs, such as Marx's political *Das Kapital*, or Newton's scientific *Philosophiæ Naturalis Principia Mathematica*. All of these works can be held to have started traditions, in one sense of the word or another, and all are remarkable for the novelty they exhibit or are held to exhibit.[13] None of them had succeeded in creating a tradition until others had adopted them. It is that act of adopting,

---

13   Scholars often examine the roots of any idea and compare them with earlier material, including some that did not have as much impact, or that later faded into relative obscurity. Among radicals (who enjoy iconoclasm), and Pagans (who often argue both against the novelty of Christian practices, and for the antiquity of their own), this leads to a habit of attempting to establish who or what "really" started any given tradition, underestimating the importance not just of proclaiming something, but of also finding adherents, without which there is no tradition. Whatever one may argue about the precedents of the Law of Thelema, or other Thelemic artefacts, Thelema as a tradition was started by Crowley, not by Rabelais or St. Augustine.

and hence of the philosophy being passed on, that makes the tradition.

Another notable point about traditions, is that they are generally created by "great" men and women. This is tautologous—creating a tradition with many adherents will afford you a place in the history books, developing an idea that is roundly ignored will result in obscurity—but still significant. Most people do not believe they are capable of producing a best-selling book, or leading a political party, or any other act that will affect a large number of people to a degree comparable to the founding of a tradition. Those that do so tend to experience anxiety in their attempts for fame, or merely arrive at fame while pursuing other goals. We would expect someone who set out to deliberately found a new tradition to exhibit a very high sense of self-efficacy.

Sanders may have set himself outside of the Gardnerian tradition, but in doing so perhaps more found himself *with* a tradition, than having consciously *created* one. He also felt the need to reduce, rather than to glory in, his position of founder, through his referencing his grandmother as a source. And this from a man who clearly had a high sense of self-efficacy, which was as needed to deal with the role that he *did* claim.

Probably the earliest completely self-concious attempts to create a Wiccan tradition was Buckland's creation of Seax-Wica [Buckland 1974], which Buckland attempted when he had already attained a considerable measure of accomplishment, and could be justified in such a view of his own abilities.

By the end of the 1990s, young newcomers to Innovative Witchcraft, even those who considered themselves to be lacking in experience, could not only harbour ambitions of starting a new tradition, but could quite openly express such an ambition, and expect it to be accepted, and perhaps even commended as a goal that would be beneficial to their form of Craft. One 20-year-old Witchvox.com contributor's biographical notes, for example, reads "After gaining more experience with groups, I plan on starting a tradition of my own once I start my family in a few years' time" [Camaralzman 2002]. The positioning of this plan with other plans for her life, starting a family, would suggest that starting a tradition is seen as a considerable undertaking, but no more so than very common ambitions, such as raising a family, developing a house, a particular career plan, or any other long term goal. This goal is catered for directly by Raven Grimassi's *Crafting Wiccan Traditions* [Grimassi 2008], which suggests the ambition is widespread enough for those who harbour it to count as a market.

It is clear that by this stage, Innovative Witchcraft has inherited the term *tradition* from Traditional Wicca, but is using it almost purely as a term denoting denominations; and it is spawning such denominations at a tremendous rate. These two features, the change in definition and the proliferation of denominations, are clearly linked, but worth considering separately.

For different trends in Innovative Witchcraft to spread rapidly is inevitable given the the very value on innovation that it exhibits, and the isolation between developing practices. The question then, is not why such groups differ in their practices and beliefs, as why do they identify as a denomination or tradition at all?

One possible influence can be found in the large number of Christian denominations to be found in North America, particularly in the United States, and the strain of disestablishmentarianism that influenced it. The influence of Non-Conformist Christians fleeing England for the American Colonies upon

American history is well-enough stated to count as schoolchild knowledge in North America, if less well-known elsewhere.[14] In less than 40 years, over 7,000 disestablishmentarianist families moved to the British colonies in America [Anne 2007], and this has left its mark upon American forms of Christianity in many ways.

One such legacy is the relative mobility of church affiliations, and a growth in denominations considerably beyond what is often experienced in Europe, particularly within the Baptist family of churches. The degree to which different Baptist churches are independent from each other, in line with the Doctrine of Soul Competency, could have chimed in the minds of some who were particularly familiar with those churches (ex-Baptists especially, and those living in areas with a high Baptist population) with the degree of coven autonomy held by Traditional and Innovative covens alike. Even outside of Baptist congregations, Christians in the US have always been more likely to express significant differences through schism rather than internal dissent, compared to Christians elsewhere. The progress of Mormonism, from a position of conflict during the Mormon Wars of the nineteenth century, to being a quieter but still strong influence on the culture of Utah in particular, also sets a precedent for dissenting opinions finding a clear independent voice in the United States, which could make schism seem a more productive route than other expressions of dissent.

---

14 In the Old World, we've absorbed enough artefacts of modern American culture to be aware that the history of the colonial "pilgrims" is much celebrated and heavily taught in American schools, but not quite enough for a comparable fluency with that history itself to be common here.

Attached to this is a sense of entitlement that has led to particularly liberal legislation concerning the incorporation of religious bodies, licensing for performing marriages, and so on, that may even have fed back to influence some of their religious beliefs.[15]

As such, when a group of people consider the choices that differences between themselves and their coreligionists offer—to express their dissent from within, to identify themselves with another existing group, or in loose terms (such as "Christian", "Pagan", etc. without any more specific denomination), or to schism and form a new denomination—then the history and culture of the United States makes schism more likely there than elsewhere.

With the two best-known Wiccan denominations being closely associated with their founders (particularly in Gardnerianism being named after Gardner and Alexandrianism at least chiming with the name of Alex Sanders[16]), and many of the differences seeming to be more a matter of style than of serious theological difference (particularly if one makes the assumption that doctrine

---

15 The practice of healing by laying on of hands via televisual broadcast seems a particularly American religious practice. Perhaps more significant still, is the eschatological doctrine of *The Rapture*, a concept found primarily among Fundamentalist groups—despite a lack of scriptural evidence complained of by other Fundamentalists—and in many ways comparable to a particularly American view of protected rights. While English in origin, the relatively small impact the doctrine has had outside of the United States and Canada makes it much restricted to American Fundamentalism; a spiritual equivalent of expecting the "god-given" rights of tax-paying citizens to be protected. Perhaps the climate described above made the development of such a doctrine more likely.

16 Differing accounts disagree on whether *Alexandrian* comes from Sanders' first name or the Library of Alexandria.

marks the defining difference between religious traditions, as is explored in later chapters), the relative willingness to form new denominations seen in other forms of religious expression in the United States could easily find even greater impact upon Paganism, and upon Wicca in particular. From there this tendency could be exported back to Britain and the rest of the world.

In attempting to explain the fact that the word *tradition* continued to be used, even when it no longer applied in many senses, we are offered fewer clues. The word *denomination* is perfectly apt; *denomination* in itself means simply a named unit, and will immediately apply to any group once it has any sort of defined identity, whether a Traditional Wiccan Tradition, such as the Alexandrian Tradition, a long-standing Innovative Tradition, or a new "Tradition" of a single coven.

Perhaps this relates to assumptions about what composes the dividing line between denominations. The best known splits within Christianity have occurred on crucial points of Christian theology—Transubstantiation, free will, theodicy, the nature and source of Salvation—and even those differences that were more strictly political—such as the authority of Church leaders—tended to involve at least one side of the split offering a theological argument for their position. The schisms involved have also led to considerable bloodshed in Europe, and remained divisive in the US even in the 1960s and beyond, as shown by concerns raised by a Roman Catholic becoming President [Kennedy 1960].

As such, two Innovative Witchcraft groups who held to pretty much the same range of beliefs and practices, but differed primarily on god names and aspects of calendar myths highlighted in their Sabbat rituals, and who generally got on well with each other (or even just pretended to), might not see the differences between them as comparable to that between Christian denominations, and hence not see the word *denomination* as appropriate.

A further influence could have been the lack of clarity on just what made a tradition. Descriptions of the differences between Gardnerianism and Alexandrianism commonly state that Alexandrians are "more likely" to make use of ceremonial magic. "More likely" does not a definition make. Some even go on to express the problems with this distinction, since a given Gardnerian coven may make considerably more use of such ceremonial magic than a given Alexandrian coven. For Traditional Wiccans, the most obvious distinction is in the lineage. Having abandoned or downplayed the significance of initiatory lineage, as many Innovative Witches had, the differences became either invisible, or else imagined to be other than they are.

Perhaps *denomination* was simply seen as being primarily a Christian word, and its use was deliberately avoided as such, by Pagans wishing to differentiate their religion from Christianity.

Ultimately though, I think that the strongest influence here is that of inertia and poetry. Innovative Witchcraft inherited, from both Traditional Wicca and Western magical practice, the term *tradition* and found no reason to stop using it. Also, as will be seen elsewhere, the poetry and nuances of Wiccan terminology have a force of their own from which it is hard, and perhaps unwise, for Innovative Witches to completely depart. *Tradition* had simply become a "Wiccan word," and so it was used.

2.2 The Prevalence of Craft Traditions

Since traditions, in the general dictionary senses, are what define Traditional Wicca, it is worth examining some of the better known such traditions, and how Innovative Witchcraft practices maintain, drop, or alter them.

2.2.1 The Wiccan Rede

The Wiccan Rede is probably the most widely known item from the entire corpus of Wiccan writing. In one sense this is strange—it doesn't appear in descriptions of the liturgy of any Traditional rituals, and is relatively rare in Innovative liturgies—but in another it is easily explicable:

Some interpretations are often compared to what cowans[17] know about their own and other religions, in particular the ethic of reciprocity found in many religions. As such it is often held as justifying a tolerant view of Wiccans by arguing that a reasonable degree of ethical behaviour should be expected from Wiccans, and hence they should not be feared and any form of discrimination or persecution against them is unjustified.

In its most common form the Rede is:

An it harm none, do what thou wilt.

Or in more modern English:

If it harms none, do what you will.

Other versions include the slightly extended couplet:

Eight words the Wiccan Rede fulfil
'An it harm none, do what thou will'.

---

17 *Cowan* is a term for outsiders; compare *gentile*. Due to the very differences of definition that are examined here, it is not clear whether some witches would consider some other witches to be *cowans*. Here I use it for people who do not consider themselves to be a witch in any way.

This underlines the apparent completeness of the Rede. Finally, there is the poem, "Rede of the Wiccae" published by Lady Gwynne Thompson, and attributed by her to her grandmother [Thompson 1975], which includes the above lines among others.

So. What then, does it mean?

Unfortunately this question has been the subject of much debate, beginning among Traditionals and continuing largely among the Innovative.

The barest reading would be as follows:

> *Rede means advice, hence you are advised as follows:*
> *In the case of your wanting to do something, and that thing not causing harm, go ahead and do it.*

Notably, no law is mandated, and no advice is given concerning whether or not one may engage in harmful action; it implies you are not at as complete liberty in such cases as in harmless ones, but doesn't rule out that such harm-causing action might still be appropriate. For the sake of further discussion, we shall label this the *libertarian* reading.

The most common reading seems to be:

> *If something would cause harm, don't do it.*
> *If something wouldn't cause harm, do it.*

We shall label this the *legislative* reading.

Critiques of the legislative reading will often focus on the impossibility of guaranteeing that one's actions result in no harm. They tend to result in the following reading:

> *If something will clearly do a lot of harm, don't do it.*
> *If something will clearly do little or no harm, do it.*
> *Otherwise balance the potential for harm of differing courses of action, and pick that which will result in the least harm.*

27

We shall label this the *mitigative* reading. Variants of the mitigative may agree with the libertarian in pointing out that *rede* means advice, not a law or rule, or may treat it as a law as the legislative does, and insist that Wiccans should follow it, or indeed people may state that all Wiccans do.

Both the legislative and mitigative reading will result in further debates on whether or not a Wiccan can engage in a particular course of action. In some cases this will result in claims that something could never possibly be done by a Wiccan.[18]

A fourth reading compares the wording of the Rede with that of the Law of Thelema,[19] and noting that "do what thou wilt" is contained in both, associates the two; claiming that Wicca borrowed not just a wording, but the Rede itself from *Liber AL vel Legis*. We shall call this the *Thelemic* reading.

Doing so entails that examination of the Rede can essentially become examination of the Law of Thelema, and absorb all

---

18 At the most optimistic, this seems to follow from assumptions about people's success in following the laws of their religion, that would have us live in a world where Christians never lied, Muslims always treated Jews with respect, and Buddhists never shot unarmed terrorist suspects in cold blood. History suggesting otherwise quite clearly, we must conclude by analogy that Wiccans will indeed do harmful acts, whatever someone might say about the Rede.

At the most cynical, this gives people a mechanism by which they can dismiss people whose actions they disagree with as not "Real Wiccans," just as others will be dismissed by their coreligionists as not "Real Christians," not "Real Buddhists," and so on.

At the most pessimistic, we can merely conclude that people are making claims for Wiccans as morally unimpeachable that few cowans will be foolish enough to believe.

19 *Do what thou wilt shall be the whole of the law*
Love is the Law, Love under Will. [Crowley 1904]/[Crowley 1989a]

Thelemic literature on the topic wholesale to replace what had previously been written by Wiccans and other Pagans. It also raises several problems, starting with the condition of "An it harm none" becoming not just meaningless, but a compromise to expressing one's True Will. Indeed, it also necessitates that *True Will* either be adopted from Thelema, or at least the question of whether and how θέλημα might differ from *will*, as commonly understood in English, must be examined. Ultimately, the question passes outside of the scope of Wicca itself, and into that of Thelema. Further, while it claims to be the most historical—being able to cite its sources, so to speak—it is arguably the most unhistorical, for it is the most difficult to correlate to Gardner's writings on Wiccan ethics. Ultimately, the argument that the Rede is related to the Law of Thelema never does seem to overcome the "An it harm none" part of the Rede without revising it. Perhaps it is mostly for this reason that the position appears to be a minority one.

The libertarian reading of the Rede has a limited scope, in not addressing any of the cases where ethics are most challenged. Those who hold to it may feel this to be a philosophical advantage, examining one aspect of ethics clearly rather than trying to fit all moral questions into one rhyming couplet. Those who hold to other readings, may consider it to be at a philosophical disadvantage for much the same reason. It is clearly of almost no rhetorical value in inter-religious dialogue, and of little value in arguing someone's behaviour is or isn't immoral. It can claim a strong historical grounding; being quite revolutionary in times when the impact of received morality upon both social conventions and legislation was much stronger than it is now; and so defending Wiccans who follow the advice of the Goddess:

And ye shall be free from slavery;
And as a sign that ye be really free, ye shall be naked in
your rites;
And ye shall dance, sing, feast, make music and love,
All in my praise. [Charge]

This same historical grounding makes it, arguably, partially obsoleted, or at least no longer as remarkable as once it would have been: that one must demonstrate harm before prohibiting something is now generally accepted among liberal and even many conservative perspectives, and will form the focus of debate on any legal bans on anything others might enjoy engaging in.

This may have encouraged the legislative and mitigative readings to become the dominant positions. Indeed, these two tend to bleed into each other, the legislative being held as a kind of ideal, with the mitigative as a practical application of it.

Their historical justification is debatable. The mitigative in particular offers, indeed almost requires, a large amount of scope for debate among those who hold to it, and it seems strange that such debates should hold so much importance within Wiccan discussion today, and yet not leave a comparable mark upon the earliest public Wiccan writings. The legislative view as an ideal differs from the way Gardner's writings seems to accept that there will be cases where one must do harm, without even considering that things could be otherwise; but this in itself speaks directly in support of the mitigative view. The libertarian view can address that by merely ruling this concern to be out of scope for the Rede, and also in pointing to the tactical sense in reducing the harm one does as addressed by the Ardanes.

It is not even possible to say with certainty that early Wiccans held to any "Rede". Gardner's writing on the topic of Wiccan

30

ethics makes no mention of the Rede, but argues by analogy with a work of fiction:

> Witches cannot sympathise with this mentality. They are inclined to the morality of the legendary Good King Pausol[e], 'Do what you like so long as you harm no one'. But they believe a certain law to be important, 'You must not use magic for anything which will cause harm to anyone, and if, to prevent a greater wrong being done, you must discommode someone, you must do it only in a way which will abate the harm'. [Gardner 1959]

As well as not referencing the Rede, it is notable that the possibility of needing to do harm is taken as a given, "so long as you harm no one" is not absolute, as it is immediately followed by a consideration of when one might do so—implying disagreement with both the legislative and mitigative readings of the Rede. This is considered with a lack of hand-wringing that is striking in comparison with much of what has been written on the topic more recently. Notable also is that the degree to which one may render harm in defence of oneself or another, is in broad agreement with Anglo-Saxon legal tradition. It may be more indicative of reasonably law-abiding people living in England in the early- to mid-twentieth century, than of any pronounced ideological position.

To find anyone addressing service as part of witches' ethics in a similarly pithy manner, we must look outside of Wicca to Cochrane's answer to the Rede; "Do not do what you desire—do what is necessary" [Cochrane 1966b].

Ironically, while offered as an objection to Wiccan ethics, this seems to be a large part of how many Wiccans—certainly the

Traditional and large tracts of the Innovative—actually behave. This offers that when some Wiccans position the Rede as the root of all Wiccan ethics—as some of the Traditional and many of the Innovative do—those who do not do so are not necessarily in tacit agreement, but may actively disagree. Or it may sometimes be a case of a group's concious ideology being at odds with less well-elucidated (perhaps even subliminally held) values it also holds.

If we consider the Rede to not hold this position of a core ethical dictate, which is a possibility offered by all the readings, but most readily by the libertarian, then the possibility is raised of the existence of other sources of Wiccan ethics. Ironically therefore, the libertarian reading, in best-allowing for other ethical considerations to have greater value, can potentially result in a more restrictive overall ethic than the others. It is not hard to see an ethical imperative in the Charge, particularly where it says:

> Keep pure your highest ideal;
> Strive ever towards it;
> Let naught stop you, or turn you aside;

And there are also ethical implications to the lines:

> And therefore let there be beauty and strength,
> power and compassion,
> honour and humility,
> mirth and reverence within you. [Charge]

Ethical considerations relating to the Ardanes, to coven authority, and to oaths also change according to whether one places the Rede in this core position. Positioned so, it potentially allows for these ethical considerations to be overridden, but otherwise it does not.

Considering the Rede not to have such a central position goes against what is probably now the mainstream view of Wicca, not only within witchcraft but also outside of it. Fiction writers can depend upon it being well-enough known that they can have a cowan character, with no special interest in religion or the occult, condemn a fictional self-described Wiccan for failing to obey it [Renshaw 2007].

Finally, in considering that Gardner's comments on King Pasoule—the closest he comes to mentioning the Rede—are given as a view "witches are inclined to", we are left to consider that some may hold the Rede to be descriptive rather than imperative; that Wiccans may tend to follow the Rede, but there is nothing to say that they have to.

Such descriptive readings in turn fall into two camps. Gardner's description is observational rather than definitive, in his stating that "witches are inclined to" such an attitude, and in his general claim to be describing a group of witches that he became acquainted with, rather than any other witches that may have existed. Another form of descriptive use of the Rede makes it definitive of Wicca, or often of witches or even all Pagans. Scott Cunningham's *The Truth About Witchcraft Today* [Cunningham 1988b] goes so far as arguing that all folk magical traditions ascribed to a similar view to the legislative and mitigative readings of the Rede. Casual surveys of folk magic tends to find that, following a large number of cures for various diseases and ailments, the best represented practices are love charms, ways to escape bad fortune by passing it onto another, ways to curse another, and generally a large number of acts which many

33

Wiccans would consider unethical, however they may view the Rede. But this has not stopped the Rede from being pushed back, not just in Wiccan history, but in all proletarian occult history.

Opinions in all these regards are not clearly split along Innovative and Traditional lines. Nor are they always easy to determine. The Farrars open a discussion of ethics by quoting the Rede, but largely ignore it from that point on [Farrar & Farrar 1984]. Does their opening with the Rede mean they agree it is a central tenet, or does their focusing elsewhere mean they don't see it as such?

The main difference between Innovative and Traditional practitioners in this regard is not which reading they hold to, if any, or indeed if they hold to yet another. Rather it is in the primacy the Rede holds in descriptions of their Craft. Traditional descriptions *often* mention the Rede, while Innovative descriptions almost *always* do so. Similarly, the ongoing debate on interpretations and their implications is common among the Traditional but much more so among the Innovative. It would seem that the Rede is important to both, but while it is seen as holding a core position by many Traditional Wiccans, that view is popular to near-typicality among Innovative Witches.

2.2.2 Wiccan Prehistory

As stated above, debates on the extent to which Gardner learned, adapted, or invented both Wicca as a whole, and individual elements of Wiccan practice, are not in themselves of direct importance to this work. That there *are* such debates though, *does* have an impact.

There isn't a strong consensus among either Traditional or Innovative practitioners in this regard, though those who tend towards the more absolute position that Gardner invented Wicca out of whole cloth, would certainly be more prevalent among the latter than the former.

A more significant difference is in terms of perceived implications of the positions in the debate, which in turn relate to how traditions themselves are perceived. To a Traditional view, the origin of a tradition is not of as much importance as the tradition itself. Whether a tradition dates to Gardner or more recently still, or whether it pre-dates him, does not impact upon it being a tradition. To some who may wish to adopt traditions, this may not be of any significance either. To those, though, who see the continuance of tradition as important, but argue innovations by Gardner (or those that followed him, whether within the Gardnerian Tradition, or in one of the other Traditional Wiccan Traditions, such as Sanders) as not part of the "original" tradition, the matter of just what those innovations were, gains considerably more importance.

The question similarly gains importance as a rhetorical trope that can be used to justify differences from Traditional practice, while maintaining a claim to be continuing a wider tradition. While some claims to demonstrate an innovation during Gardner's time will produce evidence for the claim (for example, by showing the source of a wording, which opens the possibility that not only the wording was novel, but also the underlying practice) other claims do not. In particular, should an aspect of practice not be found in a relatively long-established form of witchcraft which differs from Gardner's practices (and, for example, Cochrane's practice is very different in many ways) this offers the argument that one is continuing the "real" practice while abandoning the aspect in question.

2.2.3 Tools

Comparing the use of tools between different Traditions requires us first to define just what is and what isn't a tool. This is less obvious than it might at first appear; while Traditional Wicca has eight tools—athamé[20], sword, wand, scourge, censer, pentacle, cords, and boline[21]—the exclusion of the cup from that list has been explained by Gardner as being for security reasons only [Gardner 1954], and there are also several other items commonly used in at least some cases. To any external view, the distinction between one of these items and a tool may not be clear, though to muddy the distinction is to abandon one of the subtler inheritances of Traditional Wicca. Within Innovative Witchcraft, there is often even less of a distinction as to just what is considered a tool and what isn't; with items, particularly those such as cauldrons and besoms[22] that popular culture also associates with witchcraft, being elevated to equal footing with such tools as the athamé and pentacle.

While the elemental associations of the athamé, wand, cup, and pentacle[23] gives those four a particular importance in some Innovative traditions, yet others downplay or remove one or more of these, particularly in treating the athamé and wand as interchangeable, and hence removing the need to have both.

Traditional Wiccan Traditions have set markings for many of the tools [Gardner 1954]. While Traditional Wiccans will often

---

20 Also known as *the black-handled knife* though some would not consider the colour of the handle important. Its uses are generally purely ritualized, without it being used to cut.
21 White-handled knife; a sharp knife used for any cutting or carving.
22 A broom made of twigs bound to a stick.
23 Whether these associations are with air, fire, water, and earth respectively or with fire, air, water, and earth, differs between traditions.

personalize tools beyond these, and may even opt to depart from these traditions (or mark the tools temporarily, and then remove the markings after consecration, following traditional advice on avoiding detection), these markings are seen as definitely part of the tradition, even when departed from.

Innovative Witchcraft, in comparison, generally lacks any such passing of traditional markings, though groups may adopt some as communal badges or shibboleths. While markings may be taken from published descriptions of Traditional Wicca, or such magical works as *The Lesser Key of Solomon*, in general Innovative Witch writers encourage purely personal markings such as one's name in a magical alphabet. Traditional Wiccan writers are likely to suggest much the same thing [Buckland 1986], as it would correspond with the practice of personalizing tools beyond traditional markings, and allow them to talk of the traditional practice without divulging Tradition-specific details of those markings.

In both Traditional and Innovative Witchcraft, there is value seen in creating one's own tools were possible. In purely subjective terms, Innovative Witchcraft seems to me to both highlight the advantages to a greater extent, while also being most responsible for the creation of a market in manufactured tools sold explicitly for use in modern witchcraft, if only due to their greater numbers.

Additions of tools to Innovative Witchcraft tend to be (1) promotions of items used by at least some Traditional Wiccans to the status of *tool*, (2) imports from other forms of witchcraft, such as the stang[24] used in much Traditional Initiatory Witchcraft, or (3) cultural borrowings.

---

24 A staff. It is often forked, though this or other requirements may vary between different practices.

In looking at tools that are sometimes dropped, or for which the traditions are otherwise heavily changed, the athamé, the wand, and the scourge stand out.

The athamé has a prime place among the eight tools of Traditional Wicca. In particular, while other tools may be shared in use by all participants in a ritual, or only needed for those performing particular roles, all Traditional Wiccans will have their own athamé, generally from at least the time of their initiations [Farrar 1971].

This is common, but not universal, within Innovative Witchcraft. Silver Ravenwolf includes the athamé amongst her list of tools, but notes: "I do not use mine very often as I look upon knives in general as potentially harmful items, even in the kitchen" [Ravenwolf 1993] which suggests its place in her practice is so different to its place in Traditional Wicca as to be unrecognisable. She goes on to say that the "wand and the athame are basically interchangeable". Arin Murphy-Hiscock meanwhile states, "Wiccans tend to use a wand or an athame, but not both" [Murphy-Hiscock 2005]. This perhaps says as much about ambiguity over the use of the wand as it does attitudes towards athamés. Of those who state this view of the two as completely interchangeable, most seem to favour the wand, though Gary Cantrell states that "the wand is something I have never used" [Cantrell 2001]. It's also notable in Murphy-Hiscock's case, that she then goes on to say, "Some prefer the wand because it is less aggressive" and has previously stated, "Some solitary Wiccans don't like using a knife at all; they feel that it is an aggressive weapon with no place in the loving practice of Wicca" [Murphy-Hiscock 2005]. This distaste for blades will obviously weigh heavily on how extensively athamés are used in someone's practice.

As well as having a less prominent place in some Innovative practice, there are two common differences in use between Traditional and some Innovative practitioners that are worth noting.

The first is the question of whether athamés should be blunt or sharp. That Stewart Farrar mentions the practicality of having a dull blade while he was still working with Alex and Maxine Sanders, would suggest that this mundane consideration was made, at least, relatively early in the Alexandrian Tradition, and perhaps by other Traditions as well. At the same time, he does still talk of people wishing to keep their athamé sharp to be "traditional" [Farrar 1971], which would seem to imply strongly that this dulling is purely a practical matter, and hence while it may be the norm, or even mandated within some covens, this dullness is not inherent to, or typical of, athamés. Indeed, the very description of keeping a blade sharp as "traditional" would suggest the opposite, with dulling being very much a concession to legal or safety concerns.[25]

For the most part, both Traditional and Innovative practitioners seem to share this view; dull blades are the norm, but this dullness is purely for practical reasons. The distinction is made less clear in some Innovative writings though; athamés are often described as "normally dull" but no reason is given, leaving a reader to perhaps surmise that this relates to properties of the athamé itself. Some descriptions are confusing in this regard; one author describes an athamé plainly as "a black-handled knife

---

25 Some who insist on using a sharp knife will maintain that a blunt blade can in many ways be more dangerous than a well-handled sharp one.

with a dull or blunt double-edged blade," but then goes on to say "The blade will rarely, if ever, need to be sharpened because the athame is exclusively a ceremonial ritual tool and rarely actually cuts any kind of physical object" [Nock 2005]. This contradicts, since surely a deliberately dull blade is not rarely sharpened, but never sharpened, and never, rather than rarely, cuts a physical object; a never-sharpened blade may be so deliberately, but a rarely-sharpened blade is merely a neglected one. Perhaps she is considering those of differing practice when she writes of them "rarely" being sharp, but if so, then this has not been made clear.

Descriptions of athamés as always being dull are more common on the web [Andreanna 1999, Dragonmoondesigns 1996, and Tiamat 1998], with one page actually describing the author as going against tradition because she sharpens hers while "This knife is traditionally never sharp" [Twilight 2006].

Again, it is worth emphasising that dull blades are the norm among both Innovative and Traditional practitioners, while opting for sharp blades remains far from unheard of among either. The difference is in how some see such dullness as typical rather than merely common.

A bigger difference is in the material of the blades. Ferrous blades are the norm for both Innovative and Traditional use. But while some Traditional writers may concede the use of non-ferrous blades [Farrar & Farrar 1984], it is generally a concession rather than an accepted practice amongst them, and many will quite firmly insist on steel. Not using steel is much more common among Innovative practitioners, and indeed non-ferrous blades are mandated by some Innovative Traditions.

That iron has different magical properties to other metals, has long been held. Pliny the Elder writing circa 77 CE remarked:

40

Iron is employed in medicine for other purposes besides that of making incisions. For if a circle is traced with iron, or a pointed weapon is carried three times round them, it will preserve both infant and adult from all noxious influences: if nails, too, that have been extracted from a tomb, are driven into the threshold of a door, they will prevent night-mare.

At the same time, just as the properties it was held to possess made it particularly suitable for some purposes, so they made it particularly unsuitable for others:

Similar to savin is the herb known as "selago." Care is taken to gather it without the use of iron, the right hand being passed for the purpose through the left sleeve of the tunic, as though the gatherer were in the act of committing a theft. The clothing too must be white, the Feet bare and washed clean, and a sacrifice of bread and wine must be made before gathering it: it is carried also in a new napkin. The Druids of Gaul have pretended that this plant should be carried about the person as a preservative against accidents of all kinds, and that the smoke of it is extremely good for all maladies of the eyes. [Pliny 77]

Of particular note here is the warding, apotropaic, qualities attributed to iron—ferrous metal is held to offer power over spirits—and that Pliny associates the use of selago, with its requirement of being picked without the use of iron, with the Druids. The Druids are even better known, again through the writings of Pliny, for their use of "golden sickles" in gathering mistletoe. While many have cast doubt upon the value of Pliny as a source on the Druids [Sutton & Mann 2000, Hutton 2003, Hutton 2007], the association with the Druids, and hence with "Celtic" traditions, has influenced Traditions that associate

41

themselves with the Celts or the countries of the Celtic Fringe. Further, we can see the apotropaic quality of ferrous materials mentioned with particular regard to fairies, in Frazer's *The Golden Bough*: "in the Highlands of Scotland the great safeguard against the elfin race is iron, or, better yet, steel." This would clearly bias those who are inclined to see fairies in a particularly positive manner to avoid all use of it.

Yet this very same quality is exactly why one may wish to make use of it. Frazer above is, after all, giving a reason why steel is carried in the Highlands, not a reason why it is avoided, even though taboos on iron are his main concern in the chapter in question. The breadth of his survey of iron being so prized, makes it worth quoting more extensively:

> But the disfavour in which iron is held by the gods and their ministers has another side. Their antipathy to the metal furnishes men with a weapon which may be turned against the spirits when occasion serves. As their dislike of iron is supposed to be so great that they will not approach persons and things protected by the obnoxious metal, iron may obviously be employed as a charm for banning ghosts and other dangerous spirits. And often it is so used. Thus in the Highlands of Scotland the great safeguard against the elfin race is iron, or, better yet, steel. The metal in any form, whether as a sword, a knife, a gun-barrel, or what not, is all-powerful for this purpose. Whenever you enter a fairy dwelling you should always remember to stick a piece of steel, such as a knife, a needle, or a fish-hook, in the door; for then the elves will not be able to shut the door till you come out again. So, too, when you have shot a deer and are bringing it home at night, be sure to thrust a knife into the carcass, for that keeps the fairies from laying their weight on it. A knife or nail in your pocket is quite enough

to prevent the fairies from lifting you up at night. Nails in the front of a bed ward off elves from women "in the straw" and from their babes; but to make quite sure it is better to put the smoothing-iron under the bed, and the reaping-hook in the window. If a bull has fallen over a rock and been killed, a nail stuck into it will preserve the flesh from the fairies. Music discoursed on a Jew's harp keeps the elfin women away from the hunter, because the tongue of the instrument is of steel. In Morocco iron is considered a great protection against demons; hence it is usual to place a knife or dagger under a sick man's pillow. [Frazer 1922]

And indeed he goes on, though the above should suffice. As well as demonstrating the wide extent, and hence the normalcy, of such uses of ferrous metal, this is notable in two further ways. Firstly, it demonstrates that deliberately *avoiding* contact with fairies is the norm in folk traditions. Secondly, it shows that while iron was frequently taboo amongst priesthoods, it was a taboo that was deliberately broken by some. To use iron religiously or magically is to deal with the other worlds in a manner in which one does not supplicate to the forces of other planes, but deals with them actively and assertively, and perhaps even aggressively. It is to not just act as a priest, but also to act as a magician.[26]

Either extreme, of avoiding the use of ferrous metal, or of always using it, are both reasonable reactions to the implications of this view of iron's qualities, as also are many more moderate views. It is clear though, that the wider extremes are not easily reconciled.

---

26 If someone wanted to determine a term for a magician who deliberately broke priestly taboos he or she might well, depending on their own prejudices, arrive at the word *witch*.

In practice of course, many will be influenced merely by what they have read or observed from others as to how things are done, rather than by examining arguments for them. Steel appears to remain the norm amongst post-Gardnerian witchcraft generally, simply because it is the norm in Traditional Wicca, and because steel is the most frequently used metal by bladesmiths working with mundane purposes in mind. Those who are influenced by another tradition, such as Feri, by some forms of Druidy, or by a deliberate attempt to appease fairies, are therefore in the minority, and as such more likely to explicitly state a reason for avoiding ferrous materials. This is not always the case; Sirona Knight, in *Faery Magick*, states simply that, "the athame is a knife without iron or steel that is used to cut the magick Circle" [Knight 2002], without being explicit that this non-ferrous requirement comes from the focus she has on fairies, and not a more general rule in witchcraft or magic.

An implication of those traditions that forbid the use of iron, is that they deal differently with fairies, and similar spirits, than do Traditional Wiccans and others who make use of iron. This is plainly true, but where a difference of opinion may arise is in how great this difference is. Those who make use of iron and steel may consider themselves on good terms with fairies, while some who forbid the use of iron may not consider this possible.

An extension of this aversion to anything that could be used as a weapon against fairies, could be an aversion to anything that could be viewed primarily, or at all, as a weapon of any sort. Which brings us to the wand. The decision by some to consider the wand as interchangeable with the athamé changes not just the view of the athamé but also the wand. There is a remarkable lack of explanation of what a wand actually is; reading much literature

44

on the topic, it appears to be simply a "magic stick", with no further history than that, except perhaps in the fairy-tales and stage magic acts in which wands also appear. The explanation that a wand is a symbol of power (most often of temporal power, being much the same as a regal sceptre or ceremonial mace), authority and command is rarely given.[27] Rare too, is the probable origin in clubs, maces, and similar concussion weapons. Returning to Murphy-Hiscock 2005, "Some solitary Wiccans don't like using a knife at all; they feel that it is an aggressive weapon with no place in the loving practice of Wicca", it would appear that this is not merely ignored, but completely unknown by at least some Innovative Witches, unless smashing somebody's skull in is somehow less aggressive than stabbing them. How this could come to be can only be guessed at. It is true that even in mundane use a wand is a stylized, symbolic weapon rather than an actual one, but this is also true of a dagger which is never actually used, especially if it is deliberately blunted—indeed all the more so; a relatively heavy wand would be just as good as a weapon as any other stick of the same dimensions, as it cannot be rendered less harmful, the same way blunting a blade does. It could perhaps be that viewing the wand as not being a weapon is valued, not only by those who would prefer to avoid weapons, but by others as well. Perhaps this is seen as a sort of balance between weapons and non-weapons. Or they would prefer to downplay all weaponry, and while they cannot do so entirely in the more blatant case of the athamé, and the even more blatant case of the sword, they can in the case of the wand.

---

27   This is more frequently explained in regard to the wand that is often shown in the hands of the magician in the Tarot card of that name: an association likely to be known to many witches.

Notably, while the term *weapon* for tools, common amongst other magicians, is rare amongst Traditional Wiccans, it is almost entirely absent in the writings of Innovative Witches.

That the wand is made of wood perhaps allows for a connection to be drawn with the view of Wicca as a "nature religion" discussed in a later chapter. Still, in light of the lack of more direct commentary on the matter, just what the wand is viewed as being beyond a "magic stick", remains unclear.

The wand, in turn, naturally leads one to think about another weapon that became a symbol of authority: the scourge. The scourge is quietly omitted from many lists of tools by Innovative Witches, even where the authors mention others for completeness that they don't use themselves, or are otherwise critical of traditions they describe concerning the tool in question.

Since a scourge is also physically a weapon of sorts, we would expect this aversion especially from those Innovative Witches who avoid or downplay athamés and swords. Also, in some cases this could be an aversion to associations with Roman Catholic flagellants, and mortification of the flesh—depending as it does upon an attitude to the body that would generally be rejected by Traditional and Innovative alike, including Gardner [Gardner 1949]. Indeed, it could be that to some Innovative Witches the references in Traditional Wiccan practice to "purification" and the statement that, "one must be prepared to suffer to learn," would sound more reminiscent of such Christian practices, than anything they consider fits well with Wicca.

When Innovative Witches explicitly reject the use of the scourge though, they more often draw analogy to BDSM, than to any religious practice. D. J. Conway begins a criticism of its use through the reliable trope of claiming that Gardner invented it, and then goes on to explain his supposed motives: "The scourge is not a traditional Witch tool and probably was invented by Gerald Gardner, who seemed to like scourgings," and later "In my opinion, Gardner seems to have been obsessed with nudity, sex, and scourging, traits that may not have appeal to other Witches" [Conway 2001]. A. J. Drew, writing not just about the scourge, but including it in a highly speculative psychosexual profile of much Gardnerian practice, that he goes on to denounce, goes so far as to pronounce that Gardner was, "topping from the bottom" [Drew 2002], which is a two-fronted attack, since he brings Gardner in line for condemnation from both those who disapprove of BDSM, and from the many in the BDSM community who have at least a degree of disdain for the person in the submissive role in such a relationship or encounter having too much say over how things proceed. Drew takes care to state that he is not opposed to BDSM itself, though this tolerance seems of minimal value since he has just objected to the same sexual interests in someone upon no evidence apart from the circular argument that Gardner must have an interest in BDSM because of the use of the scourge and binding, and that the reason for the scourge and binding must be due to his interest in BDSM.[28]

Such an analysis of the purpose of the scourge can only be justified[29] if there were no other plausible reasons. It therefore

---

28 Hutton used the more straightforward approach to trying to deduce some-one's sexual interests of examining his choice in erotica. The conclusion was that there was no evidence of any such preference. [Hutton 1999]

29 Robert Cochrane made much the same allegation [Cochrane 1966a], but given his much-stated antipathy towards Wicca he would be motivated to see things in the worse possible light, while those who identify themselves as Wiccan should surely be motivated otherwise, which makes the allega-tions more remarkable in such cases.

makes sense to examine the scourge along the same lines that other elements of Wicca have also been regularly examined in books by Innovative Witches, and books by Traditional Wiccans that reached a wide audience.

One popular approach is to look at Palaeopagan practices. That is to say, pagan practices documented before the coming of Christianity. In doing so, scourging and comparable whippings of various types can be found, of which the flogging of women by men on Lupercalia stands out as a cross-gender fertility rite. Another example is the evidence, from the Villa of the Mysteries in Pompeii, that scourging was used in the Eleusian Mysteries, which clearly stands out as particularly analogous to an Initiatory Mystery Tradition like Traditional Wicca. Yet another analogy would be to the crook and flail that symbolized pharaonic authority. Since the reason for the flail being combined with the crook—which represented the Pharaoh's role as provider and hence the merciful side of his authority—was that the Egyptians used flails to hurt prisoners and slaves—and hence representing the severe side of his authority—in which use it is essentially a scourge.

Another popular approach is to look at contemporary or recent folk practices, especially if they are already held to have pre-Christian origins. An obvious example here would be the Czech tradition of *pomlázka*, which is popularly[30] held to originate in Lupercalia.

Another common approach is to look at claimed empirical evidence of effects a practice may have upon the minds or bodies

30 By which I mean that I can find hundreds of statements of such an association, but nothing authoritative. The association is certainly well-known amongst the Czechs and perhaps more conclusive scholarship on the matter is available in the Czech language.

of practitioners. While this is one point where BDSM does allow an analogy—in terms of the altered state of mind referred to as *subspace*[31]—this is nowhere explored by such Innovative writings, and an analogy to Wiccan practice would be quite a stretch. Moreover, a much more compelling analogy can be drawn to the long-standing traditional use of the *vihta* in Finnish saunas.

Yet another popular approach, is to compare a practice with those found in other religions. While the use of scourging in mediaeval Catholicism may be seen as an inappropriate comparison by Innovative and Traditional alike, there are plenty of uses of much more painful ordeals than a light scourging to be found throughout the world. The Sundance ceremony stands out as often involving privations that would make even a much more severe scourging than is ever found in Wicca quite pale in comparison.

Similarly, comparisons with practices in the wider Western Mystery Tradition are often made. In this case we can look to Crowley's regular mention of the scourge as a magical tool in *Book Four, Part II*, including a chapter entitled, "The Scourge, The Dagger and The Chain" [Crowley 1912], or his listing in *Liber 777* of the magical weapons associated with the number 5 and the Sephirah of Geburah as "The Sword, Spear, Scourge, or Chain" [Crowley 1909].

A final popular approach, is to look at allegations made during witch-trials. Here scourging is found described, generally as a

---

31 An experience of a severe loss of ego and self-control, in extreme cases combined with physical sensations such as that of flying. While providing independent evidence to the value of scourging as a means to obtain an altered state, most reports involve a greater degree of force being used than any description from Wiccan literature, along with very different psychological settings.

punishment, but sometimes as a normal part of the rites [Cavendish 1967].

The above is far from exhaustive, nor is it meant to be; it suffices to demonstrate that, by the very same standards with which features of modern witchcraft are commonly justified in the available literature, very little effort is needed to show the scourge standing as a particularly well-supported tool. How can people who regularly research, and indeed publish, precedents for other features of Wicca, only arrive at a sole explanation of the use of the scourge that depends upon alleged aspects of Gardner's sexuality, for which the only evidence is that same use of the scourge? In light of all the other evidence for its place in witchcraft we must conclude that this was quite deliberate, if not necessarily consciously so.

Drew's uneasy apology towards practitioners of BDSM perhaps hints at a reason for Innovative Witches to distance themselves, albeit sometimes not too much, from anything that they feel could hint at it; that they are afraid of being tarred by the same brush. Some though, may be equally afraid of being seen as prudish (Drew feels the need to state outright that he isn't a prude, and points to the fact that one of his friends is a dominatrix to prove it, with shades of the cliché of "some of my best friends are..."), or of exhibiting prejudice counter to current liberal attitudes to what may occur between consenting adults.[32]

It is an attempt to manage reputation. As such, they'd much prefer if the whole matter could be swept under the carpet. If this

---

32 Of course the prevalence of such attitudes is relatively novel. It may be worth considering the debates that continue within Feminism, on whether and how a politics which rejects uneven power dynamics can tolerate people voluntarily opting to engage in just such an uneven dynamic. While increasing numbers of Feminists will defend BDSM, they are far from

is so, then the fact that claims of an association between the use of the scourge and BDSM never mention *sub-space*, is no surprise; that there could be such a connection between the two that actually has potential value, would do more harm than good to such an attempt to distance themselves from it.

Ironically, such a fear of being labelled a pervert by someone else's standard is not far removed from the motivation Gardner gave both for his writing, and for the New Forest Coven giving him permission to do so: "I have been told by witches in England: 'Write and tell people we are not perverts…'" and later he argues, "Nor do I think it fair to call witches dissipated perverts" [Gardner 1954].

For Drew this smacks of "the lady doth protest too much", but Gardner's statement cannot be read correctly without reference to the context: that he was answering James Pennethorne Hughes having recently accused witches of just that. And for not reading it in this context there is little excuse, since Gardner quotes the allegation himself: "Some were perhaps dissipated perverts and had shame or guilty pride" [Pennethorne Hughes 1952, as quoted in Gardner 1954].

But in this self-same concern of Gardner's, we perhaps have the answer to the question. While someone studying Paganism, comparative religion, folklore, magic, or ritual technique will inevitably come across countless analogies to the scourge, the same will not hold for cowans, particularly cowan writers and

representing any sort of consensus, and those opposed to it, or seeing it as at least potentially dangerous, would have had a still stronger voice when Feminism and witchcraft were first influencing each other, as described later. The allegation that the scourge originates in minority sexual preferences could also owe something to this.

51

journalists, seeking lurid sensationalism. While some Innovative witches may have dropped the scourge out of fear, or distaste for the scourge itself (or indeed, out of fear for their own desires if it hit upon repressed associations they personally harboured), a continual pressure towards dropping its use would come from that being easier than explaining to an audience potentially predisposed to believe a more titillating explanation. Even a defender of the scourge is also similarly motivated to avoid such associations being built up in the minds of outsiders. So then, he or she is immediately put on the defensive, and may hence not want to explore the allegation too much, for while it is easily refuted, as above, to do so must still give it expression.

The effect of losing the scourge probably has a more profound effect upon the degree to which Innovative Witchcraft is severed from Traditional Wicca than many may realize; whereas those who abandon the athamé are probably quite aware that they are stepping away from Traditional practice, the scourge has almost been "disappeared". The silent abandonment of one of the eight tools of the Wicca no doubt colours many of the other differences in such matters as initiation, the Five-Fold Kiss and Drawing Down the Moon, along with altering much else of the numerology and other symbolism of the Craft, and removing some of the signposts to the Mysteries. That it stands as one of the most common differences between Traditional and Innovative practice, may seem to be of minor significance to those who have abandoned it, and crucial importance to those who have not.

2.2.4 Initiation

Given the Mystery Tradition nature of Traditional Wicca, initiation holds a central position in several ways.

- The initiatory experience in itself offers exposure to the Mysteries.
- The initiatory experience is shared in that every initiate has also experienced it.
- The initiation marks membership of the tradition. The lineage, as well as defining such membership, can be used, by those who know of it, to ascertain that some- one is indeed a member.

Given the third point in particular, it stands as a defining point of Traditional Wicca, not shared by Innovative Witchcraft. At one point, a common position among those with Traditional Wiccan lineage was that *only* such an initiation could make one a witch at all. Now a much more common position is that Traditional Wiccans are witches, but not the only witches. While differences as to what makes one a witch are now less contentious in this regard (if still contentious in the lack of any consensus on exactly what actually *does* make one a witch), comparisons between approaches to initiation in Traditional Wicca and Innovative Witchcraft continue to demonstrate the shadow of that earlier controversy.

In Innovative witchcraft initiation may be one of the following:

- Completely absent.
- Self-initiation.
- Initiation that traces to a self-initiation.
- Initiation from which places one within a Traditional Wiccan lineage, but where at some point along that lineage Traditional Wiccan practices have been departed from.
- Initiation in a lineage that traces to a long-standing witchcraft tradition that is not Wiccan.

These last three hold in common the quality of marking membership of the Innovative Witchcraft Tradition in question, and also mark a shared experience within it. Beyond that it is difficult to comment further. Some may well expose someone to Mysteries, but whether this holds or not, and whether these Mysteries are comparable to those experienced by Traditional Wiccans, is impossible to say.[33]

The case of no initiation could entail initiation, of whatever sort, being an ambition or it being merely seen as unimportant. If Innovative Witches simply view themselves as different to Traditional Wiccans, then there will be little in the way of disagreement between them and many Traditional Wiccans. However, deciding that initiation is not important will likely be on the basis of some sort of understanding of just what initiation is. This understanding could indeed be a bone of contention.

Scott Cunningham argues that "True initiation isn't a rite performed by one human being upon another" [Cunningham 1988a]. Now, initiation in general is indeed a rite performed by one human being upon another, or upon more than one at a time. This is true not only of Traditional Wicca, and other initiatory traditions of witchcraft, but also of just about every religion or magical order for which there is any concept of

---

33　I can offer a personal experience, having been both initiated into an Alexandrian coven and earlier into an Innovative coven that had Gardnerian lineage, but had broken from Gardnerian practice. I am limited both by what I can express and what I would be prepared to say. All I can really say on the matter is that with the Innovative initiation, there was "something to it," but that it was very different to being initiated into a Traditional Wiccan coven, and that it is most definitely possible to have an elevation that does not have "something to it." This limited anecdotal remark must suffice in a matter where research cannot.

initiation or rite marking one becoming a practitioner. Even the *Shahada* of Islam, while not strictly a rite, and as something one does by oneself, requires the presence of witnesses. The qualifier "true" implies that Cunningham is writing about something beyond the form of ritual. He continues:

> Many of the Wicca readily admit that the ritual initiation is the outer form only. True initiation will occur weeks or months later, or prior to, the physical ritual.
>
> Since this is so, "real" Wiccan initiation may take place years before the student contacts a Wiccan coven or teacher.

Here, it is clear that what is being referred to is not the ritual of initiation, and hence not initiation as it would generally be understood by any religion, student of religion, or anthropologist, but rather the spiritual or psychic effects it is held to produce. He goes on to add:

> Rest assured, it's quite possible to experience a true Wiccan initiation without ever meeting another soul involved in the religion. You may even be unaware of it.

This is a bit of a stretch. It is indeed held by many in initiatory traditions that the spiritual and psychic effects can occur out of synch with the initiation, and indeed by some that it may occur before the actual ritual. This still entails the ritual happening at some point.

Finally though, after some indistinct waxing about what this effect may be, he concludes:

When the Old Ways have become a part of your life and your relationship with the Goddess and God is strong, when you have gathered your tools and performed the rites and magic out of joy, you are truly of the spirit and can rightly call yourself "Wiccan."

This may be your goal, or you may wish to stretch yourself further, perhaps continuing your search for an instructor.

In the midst of musing on how such an initiatory effect could affect someone, it has ceased to be an initiatory effect. Cunningham has not actually made an argument that initiation is not necessary. Rather, he has started with a somewhat mystical statement that the effects of initiation may take place before an initiation ritual, then lost this thread of argument amidst talking about other mystical experiences one may have, and so when he then picks up the thread of argument again, he appears on casual reading to have argued that initiation is not important, while in fact he had made no such argument, but merely a rhetorical sleight of hand.

At the same time, Cunningham does not make this statement with confidence. He argues both that initiation is not necessary, and indeed hints that it doesn't even convey an advantage, but also describes the possibility of obtaining initiation as "stretching oneself further", which suggests at least *some* advantage in doing so.

This tension, of both valuing and devaluing initiation, arises often when people try to talk about the question with any degree of neutrality, if they take this approach (that the experience of initiation can happen without the ritual). As such, it can be expected to provoke negative reactions, in both the initiated and the uninitiated, alike.

Self-initiation takes yet a different approach to the position of non-Initiates, by allowing them to perform the rite themselves.

This is a curious blend of two different practices that have always existed in magical practice. There have always been people who have developed magical practices from a mixture of observed folk practice, research, and personal gnosis—and there always will be. Nor are ceremonial practices solely the work of initiates, as people may work alone from material such as Agrippa's *Three Books of Occult Philosophy* without initiation. Indeed, it is unclear whether it refers to acts performed only by initiates or not [Hutton 2003]. There have also, no doubt, always been people who either claimed to be initiates without any such initiation having actually occurred, or who to some degree falsified, or at least euphemized, the exact nature of genuine initiations they had undergone. Some may well have honestly felt that they did not need another person to initiate them, but saw fudging the matter as a practical tactic in engaging with other initiates (some of whom they may have suspected were doing the same thing), but they at least saw initiation as having enough communal value as a shibboleth, if nothing else, that it was worth lying about or exaggerating.

Where self-initiation is relatively novel, is in how it blends these two streams. It both values initiation enough to perform a rite of initiation, yet dismisses entirely, or reduces from essential to merely advantageous, the entire concept of initiation as something which is passed, or something which welcomes the postulant into a group. Self-initiation as such, creates an initiatory lineage of one.

The most immediate question, is whether this is actually possible at all. By any Traditional Wiccan definition it cannot be.

Adopting Traditional Wiccan initiation for solitary use requires more than a few physical impossibilities, along with abandoning one of the elements of continuity that defines the traditions.

In a more general sense, it depends on what one means by *initiation*. In its being the noun form of *initiate* as in "to begin", then there can indeed be such a thing as a self-initiation. Some purely magical systems make use of self-performed rites explicitly for this, and this alone [Barrabbas 2007]. In comparison to how the word *initiation* is meant in the context of any other religion or culture, then a self-initiation is not possible. To initiate is not merely to *put in* but to *bring in*, and depends on the people doing so being in a position of already being "on the inside" themselves.

It is perhaps for this reason that the term *self-initiation* is losing favour among even those Innovative Witches who do not see the need for an initiatory lineage. Rather, *self-dedications* are becoming more common again as the limit of what introductory rite one may perform on oneself.

2.2.5 Coven Government

Within Traditional Wicca, the governing of any coven is very much in the hands of the High Priestess, with the High Priest in a supporting role to that authority. Since the High Priestess and High Priest would, by necessity, have a certain level of experience, and have been considered by a previous elder to have the demonstrated the ability to fulfil the role, this is integral to the mechanism of communication of the traditions themselves.

There are two pressures that may lead to Innovative covens operating differently. The first is that with some Innovative covens the differential in experience between the most senior and most junior members that such a system assumes, may not exist. There may hence be no obvious choice for the positions.

The hierarchical nature of the Traditional system of coven government may also be seen as inherently undesirable, with there being a preference for elected, rotated, or consensus-based governance, or some other structure that could be deemed more democratic.

A clear incentive towards such democratic models is with analogy to other contexts for government, particularly national legislatures. Such an analogy can tempt one towards the comparable analogy with dictator-led nations, colouring some outside views of Traditional covens, and those Innovative covens with a similar hierarchical structure, very negatively indeed.

Making an analogy not with secular government, but with models of government in other religions, quickly brings to mind the arguments within Christianity between the hierarchical government of a clergy who are part of an apostolic succession, as found in the Catholic, Anglican, and Orthodox communions, and models which reject such succession and base their governance on individualist or electoral approaches. That the Traditional Wiccan hierarchical model is a succession is clear enough, and despite the the term *apostolic* being obviously inappropriate in terms of just who that succession goes back to, an analogy to apostolic succession is often made.

The above analogy serves well enough in explaining the importance placed on lineage to someone more familiar with such Christian denominations than with witches' covens, but analogies are always of limited utility. It can become important here to question just where that limit lies; in particular, how well it serves to import Protestant criticisms and Catholic defences of apostolic succession into examining these analogous differences in covens and Traditions. It should not be surprising to find the analogy carrying different nuances in the British Isles, where Anglicanism and Roman Catholicism are the predominant forms of Christianity, than in the United States, where denominations opposed to the concept of apostolic succession are more numerous and strongly assertive, sometimes even aggressive, in their arguments. In light of other cases where artefacts of such Churches are being copied (particularly in terms of incorporated Pagan churches, examined in a later chapter) it seems reasonable to suggest that innovations in models for coven government represent an influence of Protestant (particularly American Protestant) ideals upon modern Witchcraft.

2.2.6 Male–Female Pairings

Traditional Wicca pairs male and female practitioners in several ways; in the coupling of a High Priest and High Priestess, in the alternation between men and women at various points through- out rites, and in initiation being from man to woman, and woman to man.

Some reasons for some Innovative practitioners deliberately departing from this are explored later in this work. Apart from those reasons, there are practical considerations that may lead to male–female pairings being abandoned or continued. Solitary witches will obviously not be capable of utilizing any such male–female pairing. Other groupings may be male-only or, perhaps more often, female-only, not by design, but just by accident of who people manage to meet with a shared interest in witchcraft, given both gender imbalance often remarked upon in those interested, and the tendency of many people to develop more friendships with people of the same sex as themselves.

In contrast to this, after solitary practitioners, the next most common grouping is probably life-partners who work as a couple. With male–female couples being in the majority generally, this will inevitably lead to a large number of couples working as a male–female pair.

2.2.7 The Five-Fold Kiss

The greeting and valediction "Blessed Be" is almost as much a signifier of someone's involvement in some form of Post-Gardnerian witchcraft as pentagram jewellery. While it appears in popular culture, such as in the television shows *Charmed* and *Buffy the Vampire Slayer*, it is not much adopted by, nor pre-existent in, groups who do not identify themselves as witches, which does happen with the pentagram, and so serves as a shibboleth of sorts.

While this valediction comes from the Five-Fold Kiss, the Five-Fold Kiss itself does not have the same degree of prevalence. Solitary use would of course preclude it, and many of the other differences to Traditional Wicca discussed in this chapter remove context for it.

Even when contexts *do* exist for it, the Five-Fold Kiss may still be omitted or altered. Conway offers the following suggestion:

> Some individuals and groups may wish to dispense with this part of the ritual and substitute kneeling at the feet of the High Priestess/Priest and simply kissing her/his feet as a sign of respect. However, I am not fond of using the foot-kissing part either, as I feel that this encourages a feeling of class or degree importance that is not appropriate in Wicca. I prefer to simply give a kiss of greeting on the lips. [Conway 2001]

61

This departs from the traditional Five-Fold Kiss in several ways. The first, is that the foot-kissing of the Five-Fold Kiss is not equivalent to the kissing of a foot as an obeisance, as found elsewhere. Removed from the context of the wording that accompanies the Five-Fold Kiss, the meaning is completely changed. Indeed, stripped of such context, it could actually introduce the kind of class-difference of which Conway complains.

This talk of "class or degree importance" of course touches upon different attitudes to hierarchy, but in this case it is somewhat of a red herring, ignoring as it does the differing contexts in which the Five-Fold Kiss is given. As every Traditional Wiccan initiate will have received the Five-Fold Kiss, it is hardly likely that the "foot-kissing part" of the Kiss encourages anti-egalitarian feelings—quite the opposite—though the suggested revision of it above could well do so.

Ultimately, a kiss on the lips is just simply not a Five-Fold Kiss, and neither physically nor verbally comparable. A kiss could perhaps stand for the Five-Fold Kiss, but only if those using such a substitution were already familiar with it in full.

Apart from the fact that the male–female polarity behind the Five-Fold Kiss does not suit all groups (in which case why not just remove the male–female polarity of the Kiss as well?), Conway seems sure that many groups may wish to depart from this practice, but does not actually give any reason why. Her work does however show a continual desexualization of practice, to the point that any kiss one would not give to an elderly maiden aunt at a formal event does not fit into her version of the Craft.

2.2.8 Drawing Down the Moon and The Charge of the Goddess

Drawing Down the Moon, where the Goddess is invoked into the body of the High Priestess, is a key focal point of Traditional Wiccan rites, making its absence from many published Innovative Rites therefore of particular interest. One influence on this is perhaps the impossibility of solitary practitioners performing it in the Traditional Wiccan manner, where the High Priest draws down into the High Priestess. Another could be the difficulty in teaching the technique through textual media. Edain McCoy's *Lady of the Night* [McCoy 1996] makes an attempt at teaching what she labels "Drawing Down the Moon" that is essentially a solitary meditative technique. With an extent of one paragraph on how to do so, and another warning that anything that feels in any way negative almost certainly can't, in her opinion, be considered a goddess, there is very little focus on it, in a book specifically about ways for Pagan witches to work with the moon. The text I found with the most to say on the subject was Ann Finnin's avowedly non-Wiccan, *The Forge of Tubal Cain* [Finnin 2008]. While this book discusses drawing down at some length, it neither provides nor attempts to provide a "how-to", but describes experiences and difficulties students learning the technique in a coven context may have, and how their teachers will help them to deal with them.

Given the lack of Drawing Down of the Moon in many Innovative rites, and the difference between it and the Traditional Wiccan form in many others, it is perhaps a wonder that the Charge of the Goddess remains common throughout Innovative Witchcraft. While many Innovative liturgies lack a place for it, innumerable variants can be found throughout Innovative writings, both in print and online. It would seem that, at least as a written text, it has become a significant piece of Wiccan inheritance, even appearing in popular culture artefacts, such as the sleeve-notes of a musical album [O'Connor 1994].

2.2.9 Feast Days

Although an examination of many features of Traditional Wicca will turn up various departures from those features within Innovative Witchcraft—and some of these departures are quite remarkable—in the case of the dates of the Sabbats. what is most remarkable is how *little* variation there is. At most there are some minor differences concerning whether Imbolc should be considered the first or the second of February, whether near-by dates of greater significance locally (such as St John's Day in the case of the Summer Solstice) should be used, and what the degree of importance ascribed to the astronomical accuracy of equinoxes and solstices. While various theories exist in the wider Neopagan community as to astronomical calculations of the non-astronomical sabbats [Druidschool 2006], and while there is much potential inspiration from folklore holidays and Palaeopagan festivals (such as the feast days of particular gods and goddesses), Innovative Witches tend to stick to the eight known to the majority of Traditional Wiccans. Despite the common justification that Gardner may have (or "must have" or plainly stating that he did), invented various features of Wicca, which can therefore be dropped again while still considering oneself to be following Wiccan tradition, four of the eight sabbats are indeed an early innovation of the Gardnerian tradition, according to Frederic Lamond:

64

I asked Gerald why we celebrated the cross-quarter days instead of the solstices and equinoxes. "You can celebrate these if you want to," said Gerald, "but it would be at odds with the climate in which we live....

We [the Bricket Wood Coven] liked our feasts, so after Gerald's return to the Isle of Man in the spring 1958 we decided to celebrate both the cross quarter days and the solstices and equinoxes with feasts.... [Lamond 2005]

There are of course considerable differences in how each Sabbat is celebrated, as is to be expected since the Sabbats offer one a framework with which to address the turning seasons, and differing groups with differing concerns will inevitably use that framework differently. The most remarkable difference between Traditional and Innovative, is that of names chosen, since there is a relatively strong consensus within Innovative Witchcraft.

Originally, Traditional Wiccans used names that would be understood in the context of English culture (*May Eve, Candlemas,* etc.), such as Gardner uses in his summary: "The four great Sabbats are Candlemass [sic], May Eve, Lammas, and Halloween; the equinoxes and solstices are celebrated also" [Gardner 1959], and many still do. The Farrars adopted Irish names, *Imbolg, Bealtaine, Samhain* and *Lughnasadh,* for the original four Sabbats as they were living in Ireland, and advised that others make similar adoptions, so as to keep one's practice local, to either one's current location or one's homeland [Farrar & Farrar 1981]. Many seem to have ignored their advice, but taken their examples, and so the Irish names are in very common use among the Traditional, and even more so among the Innovative. As such, the terms have become English loan-words particularly associated with Wicca, and other forms of Paganism.

Yule holds a middle-ground position, being a modern English word, but a relatively obscure one, and hence becoming Pagan linguistic "property" for naming the winter solstice. This left the summer solstice and the equinoxes with the same mundane names that everyone else had for them. Within Innovative Witchcraft, there was widespread adoption of Aidan Kelly's coinages *Ostara* (for the spring equinox), *Litha* (for the summer solstice, also called *Midsummer*), and *Mabon* (for the autumn equinox).

These three terms are based on a large measure of conjecture. *Ostara* comes from Bede, via Jacob Grimm, and is based on Bede's theory that *Eostur-monaþ*, the Anglo-Saxon month roughly coincident with April in the modern Gregorian calendar, may have been named after a goddess, *Eostre*. Beyond this comment from Bede, it is hard to say anything about this goddess. Grimm has a point when he says "It would be uncritical to saddle this father of the church, who everywhere keeps heathenism at a distance, and tells us less of it than he knows, with the invention of these goddesses"[34] [Grimm 1888]. But on the other hand, there is no real evidence to show firmly that he *didn't* invent them, or that some scholarly misunderstanding didn't lead to a belief among the Christian Anglo-Saxons that their recent Pagan ancestors worshipped goddesses of these names, when in fact they did not. Bede may be Venerable, but he is not infallible, and in the absence of any primary source, or even any corroborating

---

34 Goddesses in the plural, as Grimm is referring not just to *Eostre* but also the goddess *Hrede*, in whose honour Bede similarly claims the preceding month of *Rhedmonaþ* is named.

secondary source, conclusions cannot be drawn with complete confidence.

Litha also comes from Bede's description of the Anglo-Saxon calendar, specifically from *se Ærra Liþa* (June), *se Æfterra Liþa* (July), and the intercalendary *Liþa* that appeared after these on leap years. This suggests that *Litha* may mean 'summer', though Bede himself suggests it means 'calm' or 'mild'—which would make it cognate with the modern (though obsolete) English *lithe* as it relates to weather. Bede also connects the word with *líðan* 'to travel' (which would make it cognate with *lead*):

> Lida dicitur blandus, sive navigabilis, quod in utroque mense et blanda sit serenitas aurarum, et navigari soleant æquora. (Bede 725)
>
> Litha means "gentle" or "navigable", because in both those months the calm breezes are gentle and they were wont to sail upon the smooth sea. [Wallis 1999]

Finally, *Mabon* was adopted—quite arbitrarily—from the name of the Welsh god Mabon ap Modron.

The three names, *Ostara*, *Litha*, and *Mabon*, are each found relatively rarely within Traditional Wicca, while they are probably the most common names in Innovative Witchcraft by a large margin. Beyond that, other names are often adopted or invented to match particular cultures, but each of these are rare. More often, one may find lists of various names for the same holiday, but some of these are rare in witchcraft practice (for example Iolo Morganwg's coinage *Alban Elfed* which is often used in Druidry), and seem to be listed more for inclusiveness, and to encourage the ideology of actively engaging in a high degree of syncretism that is popular within some streams of Innovative Witchcraft.

2.2.10 Monetary Reward

It has long since been accepted that Wiccans should not charge money for the Craft. The exact interpretation of this varies. Some have felt that any attempt to make money from anything associated with witchcraft, such as receiving royalties for a book written as a witch, breaks this rule, [Adler 1997] or else drawing the line at any occult or paranormal expertise. Most will not condemn this, after all anyone can write a book on witchcraft; being a witch isn't necessary for this, though it does obviously give you a different perspective on the topic. Most occult techniques are practised by many cowans, including those techniques, such as astrology, tarot reading and scrying, that are most often done for a fee. Even when witches are criticized as being overly concerned with commercial success, this is normally seen as inappropriate because it leads to what the critic considers to be poor choices, rather than as them having broken this rule; it is cupidity rather than commerce that is criticized, much as often happens to artists and others who must balance commercial value against other concerns.

Charging money becomes much more controversial where actual magic is done. To charge for performing a spell for another would be very controversial, even if the method used was borrowed from a magical practice that allowed for such charging, while to sell an item that has been consecrated or otherwise "energized" leads to complicated questions about whether the price is for the item only, or also for the magical work [Farrar & Farrar 1984]. The question can become more difficult still when we think about the attention and intent that any good craftsman, especially one who also has magical training, will put into any item he or she produces.

Where charging money is much less accepted is in terms of initiation, training leading directly to initiation, or where some sort of tithing is used. To find Traditional Wiccans doing so is very hard; much easier is to find Traditional Wiccans objecting to the very idea that it might happen, along with often pointing out suspicions about the credentials about those who claim to be charging for Traditional Wiccan initiation. [Alder Stand 2004]

This is much the same in many Innovative traditions, though the differences as to what initiation is (if it exists at all) in such practices can muddy this. If, as the foreword claims, working with *Buckland's Complete Book of Witchcraft* can make one "the equivalent to a Third Degree" [Buckland 1986], does this mean that charging for the book can be taken as in any way equivalent to charging for initiation. If not, does this mean one could base a tradition on such material, and charge for passing on such instruction before performing an initiation ceremony for the student? The Traditional answer is most likely to start with stating that they don't see working with Buckland's book to make one the equivalent of a Third Degree. For that matter, those Traditional Wiccans who write books, teach courses, make videos, and so on, may feel that this can sit with their oaths, precisely because the materials produced are not equivalent to anything that will make one of *any* degree. To the final question, they're likely to either opine that nothing has made it acceptable to charge for initiation, or else to merely conclude that since they don't see such a tradition as Wicca, it's none of their concern whether it is charged for or not.

Most Innovative opinion is not likely to approve of such charging either. However, as models for the teaching of witchcraft change, charging for initiation—or at the very least for the training that leads directly to it—is likely to become more common. This is done by the Correlian Nativist Church, and given the ties it once had to Witch School, it is hard to see how it could have used that model for training and not charge, unless there was a substantial supporting income from another source.

This issue alone places the Correlians outside of the mainstream of Innovative Witchcraft, but unless they and others that share that model disappear soon, which they show no sign of doing, such a heterodoxy is likely to grow. What is not clear, is whether in the future they will be seen as being very much outside of Innovative Witchcraft, much as Innovative Witchcraft is seen as outside of Traditional Wicca, or whether they will influence Innovative Witchcraft to be increasingly accepting of such monetary charges.

Chapter Three

Books, Books of Shadows, and Cultural Transmission

"Knowing I loved my books, he furnish'd me
From mine own library with volumes that
I prize above my dukedom."
> —William Shakespeare, "The Tempest" Act I, scene ii

"Actually, they were quite right. You *could* teach yourself witchcraft. But both the teacher and the pupil had to be the right sort of person."
> —Terry Pratchett, *Lords and Ladies*

There are many ways in which a tradition can be passed from elder to more junior members, including:
- Formal learning
  - Learning from books and other media
  - Learning from oral instruction
  - Learning from assigned exercises or research
- Apprenticeship
  - Performing tasks under guidance
  - Induction (picking up elements of tradition from exposure to them)
- Transmission of mysteries

To learn a particular tradition and to acquire knowledge and skills that are deemed to be of use to someone working in that tradition, a student typically has a teacher. The roles of teacher and student could be relatively fixed, with one person always primarily in a teaching role and another always primarily in that of a student, or fluid in several ways, including collaborative research, study groups, teachers assigning independent research to students, and students bringing prior relevant experience from other traditions or other fields.

Personal gnosis may also bring lessons to individuals, which they may in turn attempt to share.

All of these methods can be found in all forms of witchcraft, though clearly only learning from texts and personal gnosis can be primary means for solitaries.

Means of communication with witches one does not work with is therefore of greater importance the smaller and more isolated one's group is, and all the more so if that group is only oneself, barring a staunchly isolationist approach. Deborah Lipp places the ongoing rises of public festivals, book publishing, and Internet resources as barometers of change in a sketch of the history of Wicca in the United States [Lipp 2007], which gives a measure of the importance of each of these to the development of witchcraft there, and drawing analogy to outside of the United States seems reasonable.

In light of this, the description of Wicca as an oral tradition does not hold for many Innovative Witches, since they lack any ongoing oral instruction. While they do not have a scripture, Innovative Witches are very often, if not quite a "people of the book", a people, at least, of the *books*. The ease and speed with which one can communicate online, means that it is also the forum within which many cultural norms are set inside subsections of Innovative Witchcraft. While this has yet to have much of an impact on liturgy or ritual format,[35] it is of massive importance to the cultural experience of many.

3.1 The Book of Shadows

A Traditional Wiccan's Book of Shadows is almost always a hand-copied version of that of his or her initiator, or another coven elder. Its contents are considered secret, and the initiate oath-bound not to reveal those contents. Opinions and practices vary as to additions to the Book of Shadows, but these variations agree on ensuring that at the very least the "core" material that one's initiator received from his or her initiator, is in turn copied *in toto*.

Innovative Witchcraft, as in everything else, varies considerably. However, by far the most common definitions hold that a Book of Shadows is considerably more personal than in Traditional Wicca. The glossary at ReligiousTolerance.org defines the term *Book of Shadows* as, "A personal diary of a Wiccan or other Neopagan in which she/he records their ritual activities" [Robinson 1996], while Scott Cunningham describes the Book of Shadows thus:

> The Book of Shadows is a Wiccan workbook containing invocations, ritual patterns, spells, runes, rules governing magic, and so on. Some Books of Shadows are passed from one Wiccan to another, usually upon initiation, but the vast majority of Books of Shadows today are composed by each individual Wiccan. (Cunningham 1988a)

---

35 Entirely virtual rituals do exist.

    Also, while not witchcraft, The Open Source Order of the Golden Dawn (www.osogd.org) stands as an effort to use Internet collaboration for the development of rituals similarly to the development of open-source software.

The majority of other definitions either repeat that it is a diary, that it is a workbook, or some combination of the two. This would seem to be by far the most popular view within Innovative Witchcraft.

Hand-writing remains the norm, though perhaps with less justification. While the practice of maintaining a "Disc of Shadows" may go against mandated Traditional Wiccan practice,[36] once one is no longer maintaining the Book of Shadows as an inheritance within a tradition it seems reasonable to abandon the holographic practice too, in favour of the advantages of speed, ease of editing and searching, privacy, and high-grade encryption, that most of us use routinely in other writing tasks. While there are some who do so, Innovative Witches often argue against it. Cunningham suggests:

> It is a good idea to copy your spells and rites by hand. Not only does this ensure that you've read the work completely, it also allows easier reading by candlelight. (Cunningham 1988a)

The first point has some value,[37] but the second seems doubtful; it is a rare scribe whose hand can compete in legibility in poor light with a large-font printout.

On balance, I think the preference for handwriting within Innovative Witchcraft may be largely an emotional thing; there is

---

36 Arguably though, the injunction that one's book be in one's, "hand of write," assumes no other technological means of transcription, and is hence really an injunction against it being in any other hand, and the risk of exposure that would bring.

37 Though I do wonder if my knowledge of basic geology is really any better for having had a primary-school teacher who insisted upon the same technique.

always a pleasure to be found in crafting something yourself with the minimal degree of technology, and doing so creates a connection to the result. There may also be the fact that hand-writing is seen as old-fashioned, or perhaps simply as a "Wiccan thing."

It is worth noting that Frederic Lamond describes the original practice among Gardnerians as closer to the Innovative, quoting Gardner as saying:

> The Book of Shadows is not a Bible or Quran. It is a personal cookbook of spells that have worked for the owner. I am giving you mine to copy to get you started: as you gain experience discard those spells that don't work for you and substitute those that you have thought of yourselves. (Lamond 2005)

This is certainly quite different to the practices concerning the Book of Shadows that exist now within Traditional Wicca. Nor can it be explained as a matter of Traditions maintaining a practice, while abandoning the wisdom behind it; the quotation above does not well-describe the contents of the Books of Shadows, which while certainly not comparable to the Bible or al-Qur'ān, is not quite a "cookbook of spells" either. The question of whether the Innovative practice is a concious return to what is believed to be the earlier Traditional practice, or an innovation (perhaps due to the fact that oaths would prevent a transmission of Books of Shadows out of the Traditions to which they belonged), which happened to repeat Gardner's earlier practice is unclear. Revisionism and reactivity are likely to muddy the waters and make it less clear as time goes on. In either case, it remains that Traditional and Innovative concepts of the Book of Shadows are very much at odds with each other.

This can become a contentious point in the practices of sharing the Book. Both concepts of the Book of Shadows allow one, and indeed in certain circumstances encourage one, to share one's Book with others. The differences between the two are primarily whom one may share it with. Both practices allow one to share the Book with brethren, but the very differences in opinion as to who is or isn't Wiccan that this book explores, means that some Innovative Witches would perhaps be prepared to share their Books with either an Innovative Witch or a Traditional Wiccan or even to publish them, while Traditional Wiccans would at most be prepared to share their Books with Traditional Wiccans, and more likely only with well-vouched members of the same Tradition. At the same time, while both would consider their Book to be personal, in the case of a Traditional Wiccan the Book itself is personal, while the contents are traditional and identical to that it was copied from (barring perhaps some personal additions not considered "core"), while in the case of an Innovative Witch the contents are also personal, if only in choice of sources. To allow someone to see one's Book, therefore carries a more personal implication of trust and respect, with a refusal therefore suggesting that such a level of trust and respect does not exist.

The result of this, is that an Innovative Witch may ask to see a Traditional Wiccan's Book of Shadows, which to the Traditional entails a request to break oaths which may cause offence, especially if there is any persistence in the request. The Traditional Wiccan will therefore refuse to do so, which to the Innovative Witch may suggest that he or she is not trusted and respected as much as was thought, and cause offence to him or her in turn.

Perhaps it is worth noting that the most regular mention of a Book of Shadows in popular culture, and hence one that may have an influence upon cowans and some newcomers to witchcraft, is somewhere between the Traditional and Innovative form. The television show *Charmed* features a "Book of Shadows" that is personal to the three main characters, who are sometimes seen adding to it, but which is also a traditional inheritance, since the book itself has passed down from their ancestors. Where this differs most from the majority opinion among both the Traditional and Innovative, is in attributing magical power to the Book itself. Of course, this is hardly a novel concept, nor one unused in witchcraft elsewhere, such as in the use of magical alphabets in talismans. The idea of the book as magical artefact can be found in many accounts, including some of suspected witches [Hutton 1999], and fictions; hence for example, Prospero destroying his book with much the same degree of overkill as he does his staff:

> I'll break my staff,
> Bury it certain fathoms in the earth,
> And deeper than did ever plummet sound
> I'll drown my book.
>> ["The Tempest", Act V, scene i, Shakespeare 1623]

While this is not generally held by any form of Pagan witchcraft, exceptions can be found. One magazine account describes a woman getting rid of a troublesome ex-partner through the use of a magic book. The book in question is not even a Book of Shadows, but a copy of the Farrars' *A Witches' Bible* [Chat 2008], a use which one cannot imagine the Farrars' ever expecting. While such tabloid journalism cannot be taken too seriously, it does speak of the "magic book" persisting today, including by some who identify as witches.

3.2 Orthopraxies, Orthodoxies, and Heterodoxies

Innovative Witchcraft has an ideological position of abandoning ideological positions. Like Traditional Wicca, it lacks a formal orthodoxy. However, it also lacks an orthopraxy. Indeed, the lack of an orthopraxy is perhaps more vocally, and regularly, stated than that of a shared belief, with being able to "*do* what suits" cited as a virtue. In terms of *self-defining* statements though, it is the lack of doctrine, not lack of liturgy, that is most often directly commented on, and in turn often seen as the basis for the virtue of "doing what suits".

Perhaps, this reflects Western post-Christian concepts of what makes a religion. In Christianity and Islam, doctrine precedes praxis. Catholicism has the Credo as the core definition of the religion, and the Reformed churches differed more vitally on doctrine than on practice. Islamic scholarship places great importance upon proving the validity of practices with reference to scripture. While Judaism is strongly orthopraxic, the basis of practice in doctrine can be seen with the answers to the Passover questions, which all give a scriptural reason for practices starting with the celebration itself: "Why is this night different from all other nights?", and then individual parts of that celebration.

That this has influenced Christian and post-Christian ideas of what defines a religion is shown in the use of the word *faith* as a synonym for religion. Perhaps though, the assumption goes deeper than what is covered by the purely religious. Thought is seen to precede action, science to precede technology, and so on. Exceptions to this are either ignored—in practice, technological advance often precedes scientific discovery, but since the principle discovered is still seen as ontologically preceding the technology, the account of the technology will often retroactively give the impression that the discovery was made first—or they are frowned upon: to act before thinking is viewed as folly in all but a few exceptional cases. Perhaps this goes back as far as the idealism of Plato, and the degree to which Christianity values doctrine over practice is part of a Platonic heritage it shared with the rest of Western thought, rather than an aspect of Western thought of Christian origin. A more recent additional philosophical source could be the Cartesian project of attempting to build a philosophy of both science and metaphysics from first principles, under which praxis must by definition come from doctrine, once the Cartesian project has rebuilt that doctrine.

Traditional Wicca is highly orthopraxic,[38] and it is a commonality in what is done rather than what is believed, that defines the Traditions. Rather than put forth beliefs about the gods and cosmology, and then develop rituals and other practices based on such doctrines, the Traditions teach rituals and other practices, and then individual practitioners may be influenced in their beliefs from such practice, and often influenced in different ways to their coreligionists, or even their coven siblings, though commonality of experience will lead to some commonality of belief. This is not often explicitly stated as such, but it is reflected by the emphasis placed in earlier Wiccan writings upon defining what it is that Wiccans do, rather than what Wiccans believe; consider the very title of *What Witches Do*. Meanwhile Gardner,

---

38 At least as far as ritualism goes. In regards to other aspects of one's behaviour, particularly outside of Circle, there is little orthopraxy, and much individualism.

attempting to address an audience expecting religion to be described primarily in terms of *belief*, expresses the difficulty in doing so: "Exactly what the present-day witch believes I find it hard to say" [Gardner 1954].

Innovative witchcraft, by its very nature, breaks from this orthopraxy. At the same time, it explicitly does not return to an orthodoxy, holding the lack of dogma in Wicca, and much of Neopaganism, to be a virtue—often claimed to encourage a high degree of tolerance, compared to religions in which differences on doctrine can lead to heated debates, or even bloodshed. With Western thinking generally predisposed to view doctrine as preceding praxis, as described above, there could then be a similar tendency to view a lack of agreed doctrine as preceding a lack of agreed praxis.

In being an orthopraxic religion, in a society that generally thinks about religion in terms of doctrine, Traditional Wiccans suffer an impedance in explaining their religion to outsiders and newcomers. The effect of this depends on the degree to which the outsider wishes to place Wicca among other religions. Ronald Hutton has complained [Hutton 1999 & Hutton 2003] that people enquiring about his work have often asked whether witches' magic works. While this may not be particularly relevant to his research and publications, his complaint seems misplaced. It is reasonable for him to feel concerned about the way in which belief in the efficacy in magic by those who do not themselves use it often leads to intolerance. But at the same time, since witches claim to be able to work magic (which if accepted suggests both that current scientific understanding is seriously incomplete, and that what witches do should be investigated by much larger numbers of people, on a whole variety of levels), the question

"Does magic work?" should surely be the most obvious and most important question for anyone to ask about witches! And so, if we consider again the title *What Witches Do*, we find that this is a work which talks to that audience. Yet when we concentrate on Pagan witchcraft as a religious, rather than an operative, craft, the assumptions about what defines a religion lead to the question ceasing to be "What do witches do?" and becoming "What do witches believe?"[39] A similar change in attitude can be seen in minor sympathetic witch characters in fictions otherwise unconcerned with the occult who would once have achieved a justification in success in a spell or prediction, but would now achieve it in their spirituality being defended morally or legally.

Innovative Witchcraft suffers a double impedance. Since it exhibits as much, if not more, variety in practice as in doctrine, practitioners can neither comprehensively answer the question as to what they believe, nor attempt to reframe the question in terms of practice. In actuality, it seems that what they do is attempt to directly address the question of what they believe, and while there will be abundant caveats as to the degree of variety existing, there is plenty written about their beliefs.

For all such caveats, it would seem that there is a strong, if informal, sense of core beliefs and dogmas that are shared within Innovative Witchcraft—and generally assumed to be shared with Traditional Wicca as well—along with some well-defined denominational differences, such as the focus upon the Goddess to the exclusion of the God that is common within Dianic traditions. There are clearly times in which the stated concious

---

39 This is still not of primary importance to Hutton's work on the topic of witchcraft; as he is an historian it might be collectively labelled "what witches did."

ideology of a group is at odds with its own behaviour, and often with widely (if subliminally) acknowledged values. It would seem that this is the case here; Innovative Witchcraft consciously defines itself as being without doctrine or dogma, but it is commonality (albeit loose and flexible) in doctrine and dogma that is most often taken by its practitioners as being what unites Wicca, as they conceive it. Despite its conscious definition, it would seem that Innovative Witchcraft is not so much free of dogma, as extremely loose in its formation and liberal in its enforcement of it.

Chapter Four

Training, Standards, and the Anti-Fluffy Backlash

> "Bunch of wanna blessed-bes. You know, nowadays every girl with a henna tattoo and a spice rack thinks she's a sister to the dark ones."
>
> —Josh Whedon, "Hush" in *Buffy The Vampire Slayer*.

4.1 Standards and Training

In providing a structure in which recent initiates can learn from more experienced practitioners, who would generally have been initiates themselves for a few years, if not much longer, Traditional Wiccan covens have the opportunity to provide at least a certain minimum level of training. While the small size of covens and their often being isolated from each other could work against this—a small group lacking in collective experience has relatively little chance to obtain any more—a measure of caution before someone is either given Third Degree, or allowed to run a coven at Second, should suffice to maintain such a standard.

Innovative groups which have developed into an ongoing tradition, have the opportunities of the same benefits. Unless longevity stands as evidence of such a level, though, there is little to either demonstrate this to prospective new members, nor to guide the group itself. The idea of some sort of standards by which teaching can be measured, has often been suggested within Innovative Witchcraft, or Neopaganism more generally, and often refuted, with the ultimate reason for such attempts never succeeding being the lack of any means of agreeing on what these standards should be [Roninwolf 2008].

For those working alone, or who have not yet attained the benefit of more experienced members that can guide others, the question of standards arises differently. If the primary connection with opinions and experience from outside of their own practices is websites and books, then the quality of that guidance is directly proportional to the quality of those books. While many books not aimed at a Wiccan audience would be of use (perhaps sometimes of greater use) to such practitioners, the continuing growth in the size of Wiccan sections of bookshops suggests that such books are being used as the basis of quite a lot of practice.

That many find such books disappointing, is indicated by the existence of articles with titles like, "Moving Beyond Wicca 101" [Mitchell 2005], and New Page Books having a "Beyond 101" brand. Given that *101* is normally used to mean the very gentlest of introductory levels in any given subject, such a situation would be peculiar in just about any other field; one would expect there to perhaps be more 101-level volumes than any other given level, as introductory works will inherently have a larger potential audience,[40] but not to be the in such an overwhelming majority of available works as to make "Beyond 101" a selling-point.

---

40 Generally, we'd expect the experience level in any field to follow something like what mathematicians call a *Zipf*, or *power-law* distribution and marketers refer to as a *long leg* distribution; with a vast number of complete beginners, and rapidly diminishing numbers at increasingly high levels of expertise.

It would seem that there is a market that wants Wicca to cease to be an oral tradition *about which* there are some books, and to become instead a religion that can be fully taught *by means of* books. But there may be limits to how much this can be done.

4.2 Self-Efficacy

An important factor in any learning or training is one's judgement of one's own current abilities. Kruger & Dunning 1999 describe a tendency, later named the *Dunning-Kruger effect*, for people lacking in experience and skill in a given area, to overestimate their skill (generally placing themselves "above average"), fail to recognize skill in others, and if they do acknowledge a relative lack of skill, to underestimate this lack. Or as Darwin [1871] puts it, "ignorance more frequently begets confidence than does knowledge".

This effect is offset by the fact that further study and practice leads not just to greater genuine expertise, but more accurate self-efficacy. With a "101" level being disproportionately catered for by the publishing industry that has grown up around Innovative Witchcraft, one can expect for many practitioners to conclude that since new books are not bringing new information, they are at an expert level of knowledge. The ability to judge one's level of knowledge and accomplishment, is hence stymied.

What will differentiate any witch, Traditional or Innovative, is partly what he or she will get from informational resources that are not so-marketed at witches, but mainly what is learnt by doing, whether from the apprenticeship that working with more experienced witches offers, or from working alone. This being more variable than anything any standardization can hope to provide a metric for, the range of expertise will not just vary considerably from one witch to another, but do so in a manner that may be very hard for anyone else to judge.

At the same time, the model of doctrine preceding praxis, implying that knowledge precedes skill, described above, devalues the place of training, if we consider *training* as defined thus:

> The concept of 'training' has application when (i) there is some specifiable type of performance that has to be mastered, (ii) practice is required for the mastery of it, (iii) little emphasis is placed on the underlying *rationale* [Peters 1969, emphasis his].

While this definition offers a model with which one can frame a standard of training, it also suggests that the concern about standards in training is at odds to the concern about placing witchcraft onto a consistent intellectual basis. The move away from orthopraxy is at odds with standards in training, not just in removing a consistency in praxis that in itself can form the basis of such standards, but in actively devaluing what *training* ultimately means.

4.3 The Anti-Fluffy Backlash

The emergence of the concept of *the fluffy* is sometimes said to have started with the website *Why Wiccans Suck* [Goths 2001a], in or before 2001, by an author using the *nom de guerre* "4 Non Goths", and an earlier resource by the same author on a free hosting service during the 1990s. It made criticisms of various trends of behaviour and ideology it identified as common among *soi disant* Wiccans, and distinguished them from "Real Wiccans,"[41] particularly with regard to (1) poor scholarship, (2)

---

41 While the website points to departure from Gardner's practices as an indicator that one is not a "Real Wiccan," the distinction does not appear to lie entirely on Traditional/Innovative lines—holding disdain for

an eager willingness to believe in historical opinions now largely debunked (or at least fallen out of favour), (3) a hypocritical contrast between espousing religious liberty and holding bigoted opinions about Christianity, and (4) a combination of a lack of healthy scepticism (on the one hand) and a cynical unwillingness to ascribe much efficacy to magic (on the other). Perhaps most pointedly, it suggested that those it described as *fluffy* may be very much in the majority.

Starting points are rarely as neatly defined as one might like, and a general trend of similar complaints can be found before this time. Even Silver Ravenwolf, often condemned as a paragon of fluffy failings, complains of a correspondent whose practice of witchcraft seemed to consist entirely of making jokes about "coming out of the broom closet", and concludes that "Wearing a pentacle and cracking jokes about 'closet time' doesn't cut it" [Ravenwolf 1999].

What is clear, is that by the start of the twenty-first century the concept of *fluffiness* (often termed *fluffydom*), had taken hold in the psyche of modern witches of all sorts. By 2002, the website *Wicca: For the Rest of Us* [Nobel Beyer 2002] was offering itself as a concious vehicle for opposing fluffiness.

The strength of the concept can be demonstrated by references, or alleged references, to the perceived fluffy/anti-fluffy divide in works of popular fiction, such as Pratchett 1992[42] and Whedon

---

departures made out of ignorance or squeamishness, rather than departures, per se. There is also no entirely clear position on the importance of initiation or lineage.

42 This may however be read as parodying, the Traditional/Innovative divide, the TIW/Wiccan divide, differences on solitary vs. coven training, and other differences within modern witchcraft. Or it may be read as merely reflecting the argumentative nature of witches in Pratchett's

1999. There is an irony in this, since the degree to which people may reference or emulate behaviour from fiction—or merely be perceived as doing so—is in itself taken as evidence that they are fluffy. The reaction to the 1996 film *The Craft* kept large in the minds of the Pagan community by the controversy surrounding a Covenant of the Goddess representative acting as a technical advisor [COG 1995] may in itself have fuelled the backlash. Certainly, attitudes to fictional works were to become a battleground for those seeking to define just what was and wasn't fluffy [Goths 2001b].

Carrying, as it does, the force of invective, *fluffy* is less likely to ever be defined to anyone's satisfaction than *Wicca*. A key concern is the degree to which someone's behaviour is related more to fashion than to religion, mirroring concerns about hypocritical piety versus genuine devotion that are found in other religions,[43] but particular ideological or scholastic viewpoints are more often identified as fluffy than others, in particular:

- Feminist politics.
- Strongly syncretistic practices (mixing practices from different cultures), especially involving the mixing of pantheons in the same rite.

---

previous stories. It could also be taken as considering real witchcraft, from the perspective of such fictional worlds, where witches routinely battle fantasy-fiction monsters. Pratchett is after all writing humour, not polemic, and the more ways he allows an audience to find humour the better.

43 See, for example; Mathew 6:2, Matthew 6:5, Matthew 6:16, Mark 7:6, Mark 12:41–44, Luke 11:44 & Luke 12:56 for condemnation of "hypocrites," in the Christian New Testament.

- A belief in Margaret Murray's hypothesis, that witch-craft was an unbroken survival of a pre-Christian religion.
- A belief that the death toll of the Burning Times amounted to nine million.

Most succinctly, it could perhaps be defined by an inappropriate degree of seriousness; a definition that immediately hits a practical problem, since the degree of seriousness appropriate for any given situation is not something there will be consensus on in a religious tradition that encourages its practitioners to exhibit both "reverence and mirth" [Charge].

Allegations of fluffiness do not fall neatly along Traditional/Innovative lines. It is true that many trends more commonly cited as examples of fluffiness are particular to Innovative Witchcraft; in particular a high degree of syncretism, and abandonment of whichever aspects of Traditional Wicca a given author or speaker considers particularly important. However, belief in Gardner's version of how he came to Wicca would be more common among Traditional Wiccans, while those with the greatest degree of scepticism would be Innovative. Yet such a belief is also often perceived as fluffy. To those who work very strictly with a single pantheon, the Traditional pairing of Cernunnos and Aradia as public god names, could also seem highly syncretistic, and hence subject to the view of syncretism as fluffy.

There is a much closer approximation with Traditional/Innovative boundaries when it comes to writers, with authors and sources most perceived as fluffy being almost entirely Innovative [Hautin-Mayer & Landstreet], and with Silver Ravenwolf being

89

the target of particular condemnation [Perseus 2001, Kestra 2005, Nobel Beyer 2006a, Nobel Beyer 2006b, Nobel Beyer 2006c & Saille 2006], and those most perceived as not-fluffy tending either to be Traditional, or to have a Traditional background.

Individual authors' prejudices will obviously affect who and what they are inclined to use the label to describe. Arguments that there should be a clearer separation between religious and political matters, often leads not merely to an argument that Feminism should be considered separate to Wicca, but which make outright attacks on Feminism; hence ultimately propagandizing a move from a Feminist position to an anti-Feminist position, rather than to an apolitical one. In particular, such arguments often highlight the nine million figure for the death-toll of the Burning Times, unsurprisingly given the shared importance this has had to both Wiccan and Feminist understanding of history, but often in a way which is in itself anachronistic; comparing figures in Feminist or Feminist-witch publications with figures resulting from later research, not available to the writer critiqued at the time [Wikipedia 2007]. One could expect a similar anachronism in discussing earlier history to be precisely what could earn a text the opprobrium of being denounced as fluffy.

As such, the concept of fluffiness, and the backlash against it, cannot be considered so much a stream of critical thought within witchcraft, as a fashion for the identity of "non-fluffy". A fashion that indeed reduces the degree of critical thought applied to the issues that provoked it, as surface artefacts become referenced with increasing frequency, most notably in often attacking a publishing house more vehemently than the works it publishes. Despite this, it remains a significant motivational influence, in shaping the prejudices and opinions of witches and would-be witches.

While, as stated above, the boundaries are not drawn on Traditional/Innovative lines, they do correlate with them to a large degree. As such, Traditional Wicca may seem to offer the potential to seekers to at least reduce the risk that one might be engaging in such behaviour, or that one might waste time on authors or training techniques one would later conclude were fluffy.

One result could be an increased interest in Traditional Wicca among some seekers. Lacking unbiased information about any traditions, the seeker has always been in the dark as to where he or she should turn. This is itself part of the process of seeking. There is now a strong theme of criticism within Pagan Witch-craft, which could seem to many to not apply, or at least to apply considerably less, to Traditional Wiccans than to other forms of witchcraft. Such analysis is highly questionable, and from the perspective of a tradition that considers some people natural members, and some not, is a two-edged sword, as anything which encourages people to seek Traditional Wicca would likely encourage both "family", and those best served by another path, alike. Conversely, there is also a move, from the same motives, away from any form of practice using the name *Wicca*, seeing them all as tainted with the same scorn, and hence favouring either forms of witchcraft that do not use that label, or other forms of Pagan practice, particularly reconstructionist move-ments, which tend to place a higher value on scholarly integrity.

What is indisputable, is that in being an insult which apparently has clear definitions, even when, as examined above, the distinctions are vague and impressionistic, the concept of fluffiness has become an influence upon the perception, and self-perception, of many within post-Gardnerian Witchcraft.

Chapter Five

Nature Religions and Fertility Religions

"Earth comprises distances, great and small; danger and security; open ground and narrow passes; the chances of life and death."

—Sun Tzu, *The Art of War*

Almost all Innovative Witches describe their religion as a nature religion, or with such terms as, *Earth-based spirituality*. Many Neopagans, including Innovative Witches, consider this to be a core feature of all Neopaganism, or indeed all Paganism, as in this definition offered by Edain McCoy:

> When one defines oneself as Pagan, it means she or he follows an earth or nature religion, one that sees the divine manifest in all creation. The cycles of nature are our holy days, the earth is our temple, its plants and creatures our partners and teachers.... We respect life, cherish the free will of sentient beings, and accept the sacredness of all creation. (McCoy 2003)

Is this something that Innovative Witchcraft has in common with Traditional Wicca, or is it something in which the two differ? To answer that requires that we first examine just what a nature religion is.

The earliest studies of comparative religion by scholars in the West tended to divide all religion between, Christianity, Judaism,

Islam, and paganism, with *paganism* therefore, acting as a catch-all term for any religion not worshipping the god of Abraham. When nineteenth and early twentieth century scholars began to study the science of religion—to study religions, not in terms of how they relate to their own, but with an attempt at objective evaluation—differing taxonomies were produced to classify these religions. Most such taxonomies were based on theories of the historical development of religions, and most such theories seem to hold to a particular view of evolution; that changes must generally move from a less to a more, "advanced", state, rather than move to a state more suitable to particular circumstances, and hence those that share characteristics with the primitive, are indeed truly primitive.

In the taxonomy used by C. P. Tiele in his article for the ninth edition of the *Encyclopædia Britannica* [Tiele 1902], based on his own *Outlines of the History of Religion to the spread of the Universal Religions*, the biggest distinction is between *Nature Religions* and *Ethical Religions*. The nature religions start with those religions which hypothetically arose simultaneously with man's consciousness blossoming into sentience and self-awareness,[44] and continue until the development of the ethical religions, which maintain some form of a doctrine of salvation and absolute measure of morality.

---

44 Earlier theories, being more influenced by the religious biases of those who put them forth, tended to assume that the earliest people were followers of the "true faith," as God walked with Adam in the Garden of Eden, and so on. Such theories persist among those who hold to the literal truth of revealed scripture, and are reflected by converts to Islam being referred to as *reverts*, since they are held not to have converted to a new religion, but to have reverted to the natural and original religious stance of humanity.

Each of these taxonomical branches are further divided, with the hypothetical religions of the earliest humans referred to as, "the so-called nature religions (in the narrower sense)".

This gives us two different definitions of *nature religion*. The narrower definition suggests a hypothetical condition that, according to the same hypothesis that proposes it, no longer exists, and the wider definition covers much that would still now be labelled *pagan*, though applying it to modern Western Pagan religions requires a degree of revisionism, since these were obviously not considered at the time.

Meanwhile, a variety of spiritual attitudes towards nature were emerging. Hutton argues that some such trends in Britain would set the ground for Wicca emerging into public view: of particular note being attitudes to Pan, that most nature-oriented of the Classical gods [Hutton 1999]. In North America, the Transcendentalist Movement, with such figures as Ralph Waldo Emerson and Henry David Thoreau, was to reassess attitudes to nature in a particularly American fashion.

That the Transcendentalists had an influence upon the counter-culture of the 1960s and 70s, is reflected by the characters in *Doonesbury* naming a commune "Walden Puddle", and *Walden* being referenced heavily in *Zen and the Art of Motorcycle Maintenance* [Pirsig 1974]. This emphasis upon nature was to create a fertile ground for both ecological politics, and an interest in the Gaia Hypothesis, which would often extend into a more literal consideration of the goddess from which it takes its name. It would also combine with racial concerns, to create a highly euphemized view of the environmental virtues of the Americas' indigenous peoples, along with indigenous peoples of other regions, creating a new ecological twist on the *noble savage*. Much

Innovative Witchcraft belongs to this counter-cultural tradition, and many Traditional Wiccans may be sympathetic to some or all of it. While Transcendentalism itself remained a generally Christian form of spirituality, many Transcendentalists had an interest in non-Christian religions,[45] and this in itself, no doubt, went some way in making the intellectual pursuit of non-Christian religious wisdom acceptable, though such interest is far from interest in worshipping the Old Gods *per se*.

From all of this there are a variety of very different considerations of "nature" in a religious aspect, and hence different definitions of *nature religion*.

Traditional Wicca identifies itself quite firmly with those religions defined as nature religions under the morphological distinctions of the nineteenth and early twentieth centuries. It differs, of course, with the original morphological concepts, in not holding itself to be inferior to, or less advanced than, Christianity or Buddhism, sometimes rejecting the value judgements assigned to the different categories of such ontologies, and sometimes turning them on their head, so that each state is seen as a fall from the previous. In this manner, it shares a self-image with other Meso-pagan movements such as Ásatrú, along with many Neopagans.

There are also nature-focused aspects in such Wiccan practices as working outdoors when possible and the timing of rituals. A respect for nature can be found in the vast majority of Traditional Wiccan writers, starting with Gardner's writing of his character

---

45 Emerson was influenced by the Vedas, and Thoreau describes his killing a woodchuck with reference to metempsychosis; "…and once I went so far as to slaughter a wood-chuck which ravaged my bean-field—effect his trans-migration, as a Tartar would say,—and devour him,…" [Thoreau 1854].

Olaf, in *High Magic's Aid*, being enraptured while journeying through woods [Gardner 1949].

Finally, many of the other attitudes that might be variously labelled *nature religion*, mentioned above, have indeed influenced the thinking of many Traditional Wiccans.

This last does not necessarily make Traditional Wicca itself a nature religion, in any of these senses. To describe Traditional Wicca as such requires us to either, define *nature religion* with greater precision, to show that it matches all such senses, or to at the very least show that it matches those of current significance to the present age.

To assess whether it may match with more recent interest in the spiritual value of nature, requires us to not just define *nature religion*, but to define *nature*. This is probably harder still than defining *nature religion*, and indeed in this very difficulty lies much of the problem. When we speak of *nature*, do we here mean the entirety of the universe, the entirety of the globe, that which is rural, or that which is untouched? Do we mean nature as it is, or an Arcadian vision of nature as some may feel it should be? Does nature include us, exclude us, or are do we stand with one foot in it and one elsewhere? Do the supernatural practices of witches place them quite literally at odds with nature, or should we dismiss the very term *supernatural*, and allow for those phenomena so-labelled, but argue that they are themselves natural? Does a religious appreciation of nature put one at odds with scientific understanding, or agree with such understanding but assign a *value* to nature that goes beyond, rather than against, materialist understanding?

Among witches and Pagans who quite definitely identify their religion as a, "religion of Nature", these questions remain open, as indeed does that of what this should then mean in terms of

97

doctrine and/or practice [Clifton 1988]. Leaving such questions to one side, and approaching from an examination of Traditional Wicca itself, the most obvious point of contact between Traditional Wicca and nature, however defined, is that Traditional Wicca is a fertility cult, and fertility has an obvious place in nature.

That Traditional Wicca is a fertility cult may seem so obvious a statement to its practitioners, and to those Innovative Witches that have maintained this aspect, as to not need justifying. However, the distance of some other streams of Innovative Witchcraft from fertility religion, may make this justification necessary.

There are two types of practice that we might label *fertility religion*, which may or may not co-exist. One is that of operation; a religion may have rites which, in whole or in part, serve to assist the cycles of fertility of people, crops, livestock and game to benefit the practitioners. And the other of veneration; those cycles being honoured in religious expression.

The first is generally a part of both Traditional and Innovative rites, though in neither is it often held to be of as much immediate importance as it would have been when a single failed harvest could have decimated a tribe. Robert Cochrane argued against the fertility aspect of Wicca on this basis: "there has been no cause for a fertility religion in Europe since the advent of the coultershare plough in the thirteenth century, the discovery of haymaking, selective breeding of animals, etc." [Cochrane 1964]. Yet concerns about fertility are far from absent today, as is quite readily reflected in the measures couples will go to in order to overcome personal infertility, with for example, an estimated 415 million Canadian dollars being spent on infertility management in Canada in 1995 [Collins 1997]. It is also just as well-reflected by the contraceptive efforts of those who do not currently want to conceive. Modern concerns about fertility do not just operate at the level of individuals and couples, as is shown by increasing concerning about food supply, both internationally, and even in affluent countries [Leahy 2006].

The other side of fertility religion, the veneration of fertility, is firmly part of Traditional practices. That sexual imagery is used along with the ritual use of food in all Traditional rites, implies a connection being made between sexual coupling and natural bounty, which entails a veneration of fertility. This is also the case for much of Innovative Witchcraft, but only if the two are linked.

That some Innovative rites do not make this connection explicit, as will be examined below, leaves at most a celebration of sexuality (though perhaps merely a nodding acknowledgement of its importance), along with what is possibly a celebration of bounty (though perhaps merely a communal meal, comparable with Communion among those Christians that do not believe in Transubstantiation, or with a Jewish Seder). All three of these—celebration of sexuality, celebration of bounty, and a communal meal—are undoubtedly part of Traditional Wiccan worship, but it is the connection between them that makes it a fertility cult, and hence not only must these three be present in an Innovative adaptation, but also the connection, for us to consider it as having retained the fertility aspect.

In most writings on Innovative Witchcraft, I have been unable to find all but the vaguest references to Wicca as a fertility cult. Maypoles, for example, or the sexual symbolism of the besom,[46]

---

46 Conway goes so far as to refer to this symbolism as "notorious"; she acknowledges it but rather than examine this in light of the fertility aspects of Wicca, distances herself quite strongly from all such symbolism in her choice of wording.

may be mentioned, but there is no indication of these being of any greater concern to Wiccans, than any other aspect of folk culture held to reflect Palaeopagan or witchcraft practice. Raven Grimassi refers to Gardner's description of Wicca as a fertility cult, very much in the past tense [Grimassi 2008].

It would seem that the fertility aspects of the Craft were once so blatant as to seem not worth overstating, and in not being stated have become sometimes absent, or unacknowledged, among those influenced by it.

The question of how this fertility aspect of Traditional Wicca fits into the more modern concepts of nature religion, can perhaps be reframed as "How well does fertility fit into nature?" By some definitions of nature—those that consider it to be the totality of life—it fits so well as to be near identical, the cycles of such nature being the cycles of fertility. So too does it fit well into considerations of agriculture as dealing with nature, for this is where humanity most directly concerns itself with matters of fertility most often: one always sees more harvests in one's lifetime than one has children.

By other definitions of nature, fertility does not fit at all. Taking nature to mean all that is in existence, makes fertility a concern only of a small fragment of the cosmos. Taking nature to mean that which is untouched, also doesn't match well, for while fertility is of course the engine of all that happens in the wilderness, it is far from restricted to it, and indeed the fertility of humanity, and the fertility used in our agriculture, are engines of all that threatens it.

As such we may conclude that there is a compatibility between the fertility religion of Traditional Wicca and the nature religion of Neopaganism, and that one may reasonably consider a

100

practice as being both, but one does not necessarily entail the other. On this basis we can neither have confidence in describing Traditional Wicca as a nature religion, nor confidence in stating that it is not.

Chapter Six

The Politicization of the Craft

"The personal is political"
        —Carol Hanisch (also attributed to various others)

"Magick puts you in touch with wonder and the divine;
   politics puts you in touch with politicians."
                                        —Ed Fitch

6.1 Traditional Wicca and Politics

Gerald Gardner's publishing *Witchcraft Today* and *The Meaning of Witchcraft*, and his engaging the media with information about the Craft, can be understood as a political act; he sought to change the public perception of a group of people, with the intention that this would result in making the wider society more tolerant of their ways, and as such enable them to live without fear of persecution.

Even this, which has a direct impact upon the Craft, and so arguably allowed within an otherwise apolitical structure, was not done in the name of the Craft. Throughout, his voice is that of an individual witch, and leans towards the tone of someone who still had one foot outside.

Similarly, the descriptions of "Operation Cone of Power", offering magical opposition to Hitler's "Operation Sea Lion", could be understood as apolitical; all citizens were expected to do their bit for the war effort, and this merely extended good citizenship into magical work. It is a tale of patriotism, but not politics.

Considered this way, this casts light on the similar story, told about witches working to create the weather conditions that so dashed any hope the Spanish Armada had of invading England. The question isn't so much whether the story is true, but as why the defence of the Elizabethan regime would be seen as a good thing to witches. Modern analysis sometimes questions the logic of such a story, for while perhaps preferable to the prospect of Inquisition, and even more so to that of an Elizabethan English person's image of the Inquisition, the Elizabethan regime would not seem to offer much security to witches. Considered not as a political legend, but as a patriotic one, the conflict disappears.

It's also notable that Gardner was a member of the generally reactionary Conservative and Unionist Party, yet with some interests and opinions that were liberal or counter-cultural. Any move towards overt political activity would perhaps have been compromised by tension between those two loyalties, before it began.

For the most part, early Wicca stood in the same traditions as Freemasonry, and the majority of magical orders, in being strongly apolitical. Indeed, someone at the time who held liberal views about religious freedoms, such as those implied by Gardner's plea for tolerance towards the Craft, would almost always also hold a belief that religions should not get involved in politics. A Jeffersonian model of separation of Church and State, that goes beyond disestablishmentarianism, to more explicitly define the two as having distinctly separate spheres of influence, would perhaps be the most common expression of this.

Yet the image of the witch as radical [Hutton 1999] is not absent from Gardner's writings. Most notably, Appendix II of *The Meaning of Witchcraft*, focusses on the insurrection of the Stedingers of Friesland [Gardner 1959]. Being an insurrection, rather than a declared war between sovereign states, this can be more easily labelled political than any action by British witches against Axis powers. Also, one of his sources on the Burning Times was the First-wave Feminist, Matilda Joslyn Gage, from whom he took the death toll of nine million, and whose own reasons for discussing the period were clearly political.

None of this goes so far as to make early Wicca political, but it does mean that public representations of Wicca were already touching upon political matters.

6.2 The Witch as Radical

Outside of Wicca, the image and history of witchcraft had been politically flavoured since the Romantic era [Hutton 1999], and well through to the end of the nineteenth century [Leland 1899 & Hutton 1999], and this image was revisited by some with purely political motives.

In 1968, the group New York Radical Women split along Radical Feminist and Socialist Feminist lines. The Radical Feminist tendency formed The Redstockings of the Women's Liberation Movement, while the Socialist Feminist tendency became WITCH.

Most often expanded as, "Women's International Terrorist Conspiracy from Hell," the acronym WITCH was a name first, and an abbreviation second; allowing it to be adapted for particular actions to, "Women Inspired to Tell their Collective History," "Women Interested in Toppling Consumer Holidays," and so on.

Beginning with an action on Hallowe'en 1968 on Wall Street, their *modus operandi* was street theatre, combining shock with humour. They made much use of traditional negative representations of female witches, and hence of women, referring to their actions as "hexes", and dressing as stereotypical hags with pointed hats. Alongside this, they also deliberately used negative representations of radical politics; including the words "terrorist" and "conspiracy" in their name.

This is clearly a political use of the power of identifying oneself with the symbol of the witch, though it has no clear relationship to any religious or magical understanding of witchcraft. Those aspects of their "hexes" that are found in religious or operative witchcraft, such as circles, chants, and labelling cells "covens" are also regularly found in fictional representations of witches and magic, and would be understood by their audience for this reason. One chant using goddess names includes Bonnie Parker along with Hecate and Isis [Payne 2000].

Beyond merely using the image of the witch, WITCH are notable also for their humour. Using humour, even in so far as a group's own name, was far from novel in left-wing politics. Even the "Old Left" would sometimes do so, as demonstrated by the Communist resistance to the Nazi occupation of Denmark changing their name from *KOPA* (*Kommunistiske Partisaner*—Communist Partisans), to *BOPA* (*Borgelige Partisaner*—Bourgeois Partisans), in joking reference to accepting a group of relatively privileged students as members [Schlüter 2007]. Humour has had a "respectable" place in subversive thinking, since at least as long as one could reference Freud's *Jokes and Their Relation to the Unconscious* [Freud

105

1905]. Situationism, which found its greatest expression in the Sorbonne riots of May 1968, featured a particular emphasis on creativity and humour both ideologically and tactically. Abbie Hoffman, upon being convicted at the Chicago Eight/Chicago Seven trial, itself the target of a WITCH action, suggested the judge should try LSD and offered to arrange a meeting with a dealer he knew in New Jersey. In her introduction to *The Artists Joke*, Jennifer Higgie justifies the attention the collection gives to humour:

> Humour has been central to the cultural politics of movements such as Dada, Surrealism, Situationism, Fluxus, Performance and Feminism, and of course much recent art practice that defies categorization. (Higgie 2007)

All of which shows that WITCH were working within norms of New Left behaviour, in their use of humour and playfulness. For all this though, the degree to which they put humour at the centre of their actions still stands out. Generalizing from humour to other enjoyable forms of creative expression, it's worth noting that the place for pleasure and creativity was explicitly noted by Feminists, such as when Germaine Greer argued, "The surest guide to the correctness of the path that women take is joy in the struggle. Revolution is the festival of the oppressed" [Greer 1970]. Emma Goldman, having been "rediscovered" by the Women's Movement, was paraphrased as saying "If I can't dance I don't want to be part of your revolution."

Witchcraft could perhaps provide Goldman's dance. The stereotypes of the witch from the times of witch-trials almost always contain at least some elements that could be considered enjoyable, if only in the most debased ways, and attitudes behind both the imagining of the alleged crimes, and the reasons given for condemning them, would have chimed with Feminist critiques of Christian sexual morality. WITCH may have found material for transgressive fun in such stereotypes, but Wicca and other forms of Pagan Witchcraft could also provide it. When asked why he practised witchcraft, Gardner replied "because it's fun". Simultaneously, it could argue against accusations that participants were detaching themselves from serious concerns; the Charge of the Goddess talks of exhibiting both "reverence and mirth" and in demanding both, clearly entails that both can co-exist. Certainly, such playfulness is to feature in later cases of witchcraft meeting political action.

There are also perhaps some hints of magical thinking. Claims that the Yippies and the SDS were actually WITCH fronts can be read as an assertion: WITCH may not really be as big as they claim, but claiming it could perhaps make them so. The Dow Jones dropping after the 1968 hex was claimed as a victory, but it was left vague whether this victory was one of political tactics, or magical operation. This cannot be read too literallly; both of these statements are clearly further examples of WITCH using humour, but even a humorous suggestion of magic having success in political conflict, could have had an effect upon the thoughts of others. That some politically-minded people were willing to ascribe efficacy to ritual magic, is clear from the later history of political witchcraft, and WITCH's legacy may well include firing the imagination of some such activists.

Another feature of WITCH worth noting, was the degree of independence between different covens. While it has both strategic and ideological precedents in other political groups, it

107

still corresponds with both the relatively loose cohesion among those political witches (who will be touched upon later), and also the Traditional model of small, independent covens, along with the even more complete independence between different groups of Innovative Witchcraft.

WITCH were short-lived, and their actions ended some time in 1970. They were however, kept alive in the conciousness of New Left and Feminist activists—partly for the very effectiveness at grabbing media attention they achieved, partly because some of their members were to remain active in politics (Robin Morgan remains a well-known Feminist who will be mentioned again in this work, and Naomi Jaffe was to become a federal fugitive for her part in the Weatherman bombings [FBI 1976]), and partly due to it becoming part of the Feminist Movement's understanding of its own history by being documented in influential books such as Greer 1970. One of the most compelling reasons for their ongoing reputation, was the impact of Robin Morgan's criticism of patriarchy within the New Left, "Goodbye To All That" [Morgan 1970][47], published by *Rat Subterranean News* during a Feminist takeover and sit-in with WITCH involvement. Its impact is reflected in it being much anthologized [Morgan 1994, Baxandall & Gordon 2001, along with many others, including a large number of underground and "bootleg" publications], and being referenced by Morgan herself in choosing to title a defence of Hilary Clinton, against sexist content in criticism during her contest against Barack Obama, for the Democratic Party

---

47 It may be notable that the title is borrowed from Robert Graves' autobiography [Graves 1957]. This biography is notable to witches for the strong influence his *The White Goddess* [Graves 1961] had upon many in the Craft, and politically for its strong anti-war themes and its questioning of the role of class in British society.

nomination for the 2008 US presidential election, as a "sequel" [Morgan 2008].

6.3 Feminist Histories of Witchcraft

Meanwhile, Andrea Dworkin was working with Ricki Abrams, on an analysis of the position of women in social, political and personal history, that would later be published in her work, *Woman Hating* [Dworkin 1974]. In describing a "war against women", she put Feminist struggle on the same terms as the increasingly militarized tendencies of Black Power, and national liberation movements such as the Viet Cong. In doing so, she referenced Gage's account of the Burning Times, and so helped bring that First-wave Feminist assessment of the importance of the witch trials into Second-wave Feminism. Mary Daly continued this with *Gyn/Ecology* [Daly 1978], which referred to the persecution as a "gynecide", clearly defining the witch trials as a deliberate genocide enacted against women. In also citing Gage's figure of nine million deaths alongside such accusations of genocide, she enabled comparisons with the holocausts of the Third Reich to be readily made.

Yet notable in Daly's writing, is a playfulness of language and a sense of resistance existing in the very sentence structure of her work. As such, while she repeats Dworkin's positioning of the witch as a victim of patriarchal oppression, she also positions the witch as a heroine of resistance. This is even more strikingly so in *Websters' First New Intergalactic Wickedary of the English Language, Conjured in Cahoots with Jane Caputi* [Daly 1987], to which I give the fullest form of the name, which in itself indicates the approach taken in its redefining "Webster" from the name of the dictionary best known in the United States (to reuse that surname's likely

109

origin in referring to a female weaver), its defined scope as *intergalactic*, its having been *conjured*, and the use of, *cahoots*, rather than *collaboration*, to reflect the self-image of subversion and rebellion.

While this imagining of "the witch" is outside of Wicca, or any other tradition of witchcraft, it also stands outside of the purely secular as well. To Daly, the witch is capable of defeating Patriarchy through means which stand outside of anything that Patriarchy can even attach a label to. This is a powerful attraction, and certainly one of the incentives to make use of magic in a political context.

With Zsuzsana Budapest's founding of the Susan B. Anthony Coven Number 1,[48] in 1971, we have what is arguably the first case of religious witchcraft being explicitly combined with Feminist politics. Budapest claimed to have learnt her craft from her mother, and as such to be part of a stream of witchcraft quite outside of Wiccan lineage. She does however, use the term *Wiccan*, and some features, such as the Sabbats and the tools mentioned in her writing [Budapest 1976], do indicate a strong influence from Wicca, though other features, most notably the very politics that are being examined here, again set her outside of Wiccan tradition.

Another combination of Feminist politics and witchcraft came from Starhawk. While she first worked without any training, and was later an initiate in the Feri tradition, with several of its techniques such as the Iron Pentacle being adopted into her Reclaiming Tradition, she points to her meeting Wiccans, and

---

48 Susan B. Anthony was an American suffragette. As such this consciously positions Budapest's coven in a tradition of women's political struggle, and constitutes a sort of ancestor worship along lines of that tradition.

hearing the Charge from them, as an important moment in her path's development [Starhawk 1979].

In light of the various ways in which witchcraft has been addressed in a Feminist context already examined, such combinations arising was perhaps inevitable.

Perhaps the most immediately notable difference between Budapest's and Starhawk's traditions, is their differing takes on membership. The Susan B. Anthony Coven was, and remains, women-only and this policy has remained common, though not universal, within Dianic witchcraft.[49] The Reclaiming Tradition was, since its inception, open to both men and women.

6.3.1 Mythological Elements in Feminist Witchcraft

What is shared between both witchcraft and Feminism, that allowed for the two to be combined beyond mere imagery?

I will argue here that what was shared were mythological elements. While claiming that a religious perspective contains mythological elements will be seen as disparaging only in the case of a religion that maintains the Fundamentalist position that they are based purely upon literal truth (notably Islam, Fundamentalist Christianity, and evangelical forms of Atheism), some colourings of the word *mythological* could make it seem as an attack on a political philosophy to examine the mythological nature of views within it. This is not my intention here. Rather, by *mythological* I refer to the value, attached to the narrative in question (not just ideological, but also emotional and poetic— value that Feminist Witch ideology usually allows space for).

---

49 The McFarland Dianic Tradition is a notable mixed-sex political witchcraft tradition, that also uses the label *Dianic*. It is of a separate lineage to Budapest's.

Simpler examples of the same can be seen in looking at the value attached to views of historical figures who undoubtedly existed, or to historical events about whose occurrence there can also be no doubt, which have acquired a value to those of various political positions, beyond the mere recitation of historical record.[50] The degree to which any of these mythological views is grounded in fact is not relevant to my point, which I argue will hold whether these views are entirely accurate, completely bogus, or at any point in between. However, shifting opinions on that degree of accuracy, does indeed impinge upon how well they serve those for whom they are or were important.

6.3.2 The Burning Times

The histories of the Burning Times, the period of persecution of witchcraft, put forth from the nineteenth century until the end of the twentieth, are perhaps the most obvious point in which Feminist history and Wiccan prehistory correspond. It was the primary influence upon Feminists like Dworkin and Daly, who otherwise did not much concern themselves with the Craft, writing on the topic.

As noted, Dworkin, Daly, and other second-wave Feminist authors, used (as did Gardner) American suffragette Matilda Joslyn Gage as a source on the nature and extent of the killings involved.

---

50 Such events as The Peterloo Massacre, The Battle of the Bogside, The Stonewall Riots, The Sorbonne Riots and The March on Washington. Being affected by narrative as well as fact, one could also say that the mythological content of, for example, *The Lower Falls Curfew*, is different to that of *The Rape of The Falls*, even though they are different names for the same event.

Gage in turn based her work upon Jules Michelet's *La Sorcière*, which outlined a concept of witches as subversive, in a manner that could be identified with by contemporary subversives, and Gustav Roskoff's use of the work of a local historian in Quedlinburg who arrived at the figure of nine million for the number of people killed in the alleged persecution against their rebellious creed.

Both Michelet and, especially, Gage are clearly political in their motivations. However, the fault for what is now the most oft-commented-upon flaw in their work, that they cite a death toll of many millions, where scholars now estimate tens of thousands, most likely does not lie so much in blatant political bias, but in the choice of source records, and in turn in which source records were available to them.

Gardner is the first to use the emotive poetry of the phrase, "burning times", in print [Gardner 1954], and it was elevated by dint of capitalization to "The Burning Times" by Daly [1978]. The enduring emotive impact is reflected by the fact that not only did the popular folk singer Christy Moore, who does not publicly identify as a witch, choose to cover Charlie Murphy's song "The Burning Times" as recently as 2005, but he also chose it as the title for the album on which it appears [Moore 2005]. Given that some of the other songs on the album are explicitly political, and it is dedicated to an activist who was killed during an action against the Israeli Defence Forces destruction of homes in the Gaza Strip, this implies that it is still seen as a term which both describes historical reality with at least some degree of fidelity, and which reflects wider political realities today.

The Quedlinburg historian, whose work was used by Roskoff and later writers, extrapolated from those deaths recorded in a

113

particular time and place as if they could be considered averages of all of Europe for all of the period in which one could be executed for witchcraft. Since he worked from records of particularly grievous, and hence particularly notable, trials, his figures inevitably overestimated the toll. Had he extrapolated from a wider range of the data available at the time, he would have arrived at a lower figure. Even so, had he managed the feat of using all known accounts at the time, he still would have arrived at a higher figure than scholars applying the same technique today, since the larger trials came to notice sooner than smaller trials, or those which resulted in acquittal [Hutton 2003].

A figure of nine million deaths offered clear parallels for late twentieth century readers with the Shoah, and other massacres of the Second World War. This is a comparison which Daly in particular made quite explicit. This offered a bridge between a politics of personal experience, and the sort of large events more readily acknowledged by the histories of the time. It did for witches, for women and for Feminist witches in particular, what Sylvia Plath's "I began to talk like a Jew / I think I may well be a Jew" ["Daddy", 1962 and first anthologized in Plath 1965] did more viscerally and intimately for herself; it simultaneously offered an historical analogy for one's own experience, along with a means of connecting to, and coping with, both the unspeakable horrors of the century's history, and the unspeakable horrors the century offered the future, in the potential for nuclear holocaust.[51]

---

51 While Plath was not as politicized herself as many of her posthumous admirers, nuclear disarmament was an issue on which she marched (see Plath 1998), and which she wrote about in her earliest poems (see "Bitter Strawberries" in Plath 2002).

The most ungenerous view of this, would be to accuse these writers of attempting to make political hay out of other groups' persecution. Avoiding this would seem to be a reason why Dan Brown's use of the same account of the Burning Times for pulp entertainment reduces the figure to five million [Brown 2003a], resulting in a figure which is not found elsewhere, but compares with the nine million figure while remaining "decently" below the sort of numbers which immediately bring the Third Reich's genocides to mind.

Such criticism though, ignores not just that all of these authors, whether witches, Feminists, or both, were sincere in their belief in these figures, but that they were considerably more plausible at the time.

Roskoff's error is arguably not as large as would be implied by merely comparing the number he presents with the numbers now suggested. Those who built on his work by building on Gage's were working with those materials available to scholars, especially scholars who were not professional historians, at the time. To argue against such writings, or against the research of those who cite a figure of nine million today, is one thing. To accuse such writers writing in the 1970s and earlier of being unhistorical, is in itself unhistorical.

Nor is gender no longer relevant to the history of witch trials. While it may not hold true for all, there was still a clear gender imbalance in some trials, and hence one must question those that suggest they no longer remain a valid area for Feminist research.

It remains though, that the most currently accepted views of the history of the witch trials differs from the accounts used by Feminist witches in terms of the number, religion, and gender balance of those killed, a fact that is often used in criticisms of Feminist witchcraft within the anti-fluffy trend within Paganism.

6.3.3 Matriarchal Prehistory

Behind much mythological content of Feminist witchcraft lies the myth of a matriarchal past. From the earliest suggestions that neolithic cultures were matriarchal, perhaps with Johann Jakob Bachofen's *Mother Right: An Investigation of the Religious and Juridical Character of Matriarchy in the Ancient World* in 1861, and Lewis H. Morgan's *Ancient Society*, this has had an influence on a variety of fields. This concept was absorbed into the political with Frederich Engels' *The Origin of the Family, Private Property, and the State* [Engels 1884], based on notes Marx had made on Morgan's work. Dealing with mythology, it had from inception been part of common understandings of prehistoric religion, but readings of Graves' *The White Goddess* [Graves 1961] would have moved it further to the forefront of modern Pagan thought.

The work of Marija Gimbutas spoke firmly to the intersection of these political and religious concerns. As such, the belief in a matriarchal or matrifocal past was part of a common inheritance of both the Neopagan and Feminist movements. It serves as a Creation Myth, a Golden Age Myth, and also as evidence of what could potentially be achieved, as well as a mandate from history to attempt this.

Many arguments in favour of a matriarchal past have been criticized. For example Bachofen's assumption that "primitive" societies are in some sense evolutionarily "earlier" than our own is no longer accepted [Taylor 1954]. This and other arguments, have led to support for this view of prehistory to fall in regard, starting in academia, and spreading from there to other spheres

116

of thought, including both Feminism and witchcraft [Hutton 1999]. It remains though, that while the hypothesis has not been proven, neither has it been disproven.

6.3.4 Sisterhood

The myth of a matriarchal prehistory can be compared with Marxism (as opposed to Communism more generally), viewing itself as a theory of history first, and of politics second. A similar analogy can be drawn between Marxism's mythologizing *The Worker*, and the concept within Feminism of *Sisterhood*.

Definitions, and hence the applicability to this section, vary. Sisterhood, in Feminist terms, can be read as an ideal, as a description of camaraderie as exhibited and experienced by Feminists in political struggle, or in several other ways: "Sisterhood is thought of *sometimes* in feminist discourse as a metaphorical ideal and *sometimes* as a metaphor for the reality of relationships among women" [Lugones & Rosezelle 1995; emphasis added]. However, it does also have a mythological aspect, in referring to Sisterhood as something both historical and ongoing (compare with the description of myths as simultaneously both in Armstrong 2006).

Traditional Wicca did not offer *brotherhood* of an all-embracing form, in the manner that religions with a sense of *agape* do, but it does offer *a* brotherhood. By extension, a Feminist witchcraft which is women-only, like that of Budapest, could offer *a* sisterhood.

This is at once more concrete than any wider sense of Sisterhood, while at the same time offering models for how such a more universal sisterhood could be expressed and developed.

117

6.3.5 Criticism of Feminist Witchcraft

In combining two elements of philosophy, one gains the advantage of mutual support between the two, at the cost of criticism from opponents to either. The most vocal criticism of Feminist witchcraft within witchcraft has been examined above, in light of the anti-fluffy backlash. Within Feminism, the risk of particularly vocal complaint is to a small degree softened by the pressure towards pluralism within the movement, and the concept of *Feminisms* in the plural. This pluralism does not, of course, go so far as to deny the right to express opposing opinions, and these can certainly be found.

The concept of Sisterhood has been questioned, particularly in examining it as a borrowing from African-American resistance to slavery and later racism, and in comparing it to other views of sisterhood, and of alternative models such as co-motherhood and friendship, from culture perspectives other than that of white middle-class women [Lugones & Rosezelle 1995]. Taking a different approach, and considering her personal experiences of the Women's Movement, along with wider considerations, in *The Whole Woman*, Germaine Greer strikingly turns the graffito on its head with "Sisterhood does not rule and will never rule, OK?" [Greer 1999]

As well as leading to a questioning of the concept of Sisterhood, as demonstrated above, concerns about ways in which privilege in class and race may benefit some women at the expense of others can lead to criticism of the ways that artefacts of one culture are used by those who belong to another, as examined in a later chapter, and the high degree of syncretism in much modern witchcraft.

Budapest's claim that the Women's Movement "needed" a spirituality is countered by the existence of pretty much any

118

Feminist who is either happy without a religion, or who works to reconcile her membership in a religion, perhaps considered patriarchal, with their Feminist politics.

Perhaps the biggest difficulty with combining Feminism and any form of Wicca-inspired witchcraft, is that Wicca is deeply essentialist in how it treats matters of gender.[52] Budapest's response to this difficulty is to accept such essentialism, albeit in a different manner, which is often considered less balanced by some other witches, and which is certainly far removed from those that maintain the male–female polarity of Traditional Wicca.[53] Starhawk seems less convinced, judging from the move away from some of the divisions her cosmology places in human psychology in her first edition of *The Spiral Dance*, in the notes to later editions [Starhawk 1979; specifically the twentieth anniversary edition, 1999].

For the most part, the question of essentialism doesn't seem to be looked at too closely by Feminist witches. To judge how their views might be considered by other streams of Feminism, it is perhaps fruitful to take the contrasting example of Hélène Cixous. A Feminist inspired by Derrida and by existentialist philosophy, she has repeatedly distanced herself from essentialism, and yet frequently been accused of it. The debate around

---

52 This is not to say that all Traditional Wiccans necessarily hold to essentialist views, but the rites certainly treat gender as essential.

53 The common criticism of Dianic Witchcraft as, "unbalanced," may be a category error. It is certainly unbalanced if we imagine Dianic practices suddenly transplanted into a Traditional Wiccan circle or one of an Innovative practice with a strong focus on the God, and then judge how well it serves in that place, but perhaps the two are simply so different that criticising one from the position of the other is no more reasonable, than for any other religious practice.

alleged essentialism in her work, is an indication of how Feminist witchcraft may not sit comfortably with many in the Feminist movement.

6.4 The Witch as Environmentalist

As noted above, most Innovative Witches think of themselves as practising a nature religion, and this term is frequently understood in relation to current ecological concerns.

It is not surprising then, to find many witches engaged in some level of environmental protest. In many ways, this can be seen as something that has happened simultaneously among the overlapping streams of thought in which many Innovative Witches found themselves.

As coined by Françoise d'Eaubonne, the term *Ecofeminism* combines environmental and feminist concerns, and in particular identified patriarchal attitudes as the root source of environmental mismanagement. Daly's *Gyn/Ecology*, mentioned already above, clearly contains an ecological aspect. Starhawk's Reclaiming movement is very much of this strain of Feminism, and much involved in environmental campaigns.

Meanwhile, the wider Neopagan movement contains many activists with a similar interest in environmental action, ranging from the sort of quiet lifestyle politics that encourages reducing one's personal environmental impact, through to protests [Druidschool 2005] and direct actions [Hutton 2003].

These three points each indicate that the involvement of witches in environmental politics is very much part and parcel with other trends often associated with Pagan witchcraft, rather than unique to it.

Chapter Seven

The ID Wars, Teen Witches, and Popular Culture

"The teenager seems to have replaced the Communist as the appropriate target for public controversy and foreboding."

—Edgar Friedenberg, *The Vanishing Adolescent.*

"I find television very educational. Every time someone switches it on I go into another room and read a good book."

—Groucho Marx to Leslie Halliwell,
Halliwell's Filmgoer's Companion.

7.1 The Identity Warriors

The term *Identity Politics* was perhaps first coined by the black Lesbian Feminist group, The Combahee River Collective [Combahee 1977]. While the concept has been traced to the SNCC[54] [Kauffman 1990], particularly after the involvement of white students declined and their policies became increasingly not just of black empowerment, but of black self-empowerment, the idea that members of an oppressed group must themselves provide at least some of the leadership in resistance to that

---

54 Student Nonviolent Coordinating Committee, later Student National Coordinating Committee.

oppression, that "the most profound and potentially radical politics come directly out of our own identity, as opposed to working to end somebody else's oppression" [Combahee 1977], is probably as old as political struggle.

Identity Politics places this concept centrally, politicizes the act of identifying as a member of a group. Where the Combahee River Collective addressed their position on an intersection of racial, gender, and sexual-orientation identities—and in particular aimed to tackle issues where those with an interest in the liberation of one such group were still involved in the oppression of another—the approach has been applied to linguistic and religious minorities, people with disabilities, and indeed any denominable group, since once it is denominable, whether from within or without, it becomes a locus of identity.

As stated above, the plea for tolerance made by public witches since Gardner is a form of politics that even otherwise apolitical witches will engage in. With the emergence of Identity Politics, witches became yet another religious minority, with an identity from which such politics could emerge. The fact that some witches would have been involved in Identity Politics of another form would of course influence this. That Stregaria and Gay and Civil Rights activist, Leo Martello, could see a correlation between the position of witches, and those of other minorities, is clear when he wrote, "America's new niggers are minority religious groups, especially the disorganized WICCA" [Martello 1972a]. The identities that exist at the intersection of "Feminist and witch", "lesbian and witch", and "Feminist, lesbian and witch", would be other examples. Accusations, in some cases true, of homophobia within the Craft, and a desire for a witchcraft that would more directly engage with gay identity, would make the intersection of those two identities a source of political thinking that would inform both. By the 1990s, comparison with the experience of the Gay community was explicit in the expression, "coming out of the broom closet".

With its situationist approach, focusing on the experiences of those with a given identity, Identity Politics at first moved away from any element of essentialism. However, essentialism was to become important in the Identity Politics of the Gay Rights Movement, particularly at a grass-roots level. The question of whether, and to what degree, homosexuality is innate became not merely a matter of scientific curiosity, but of political struggle. While this question had political impact before,[55] a Gay Identity Politics can use such an essentialism. not merely as a justification, but as a basis for building just such a sense of a "Gay identity" that goes beyond mere choice of sexual partners, and builds a definition of the Gay community from that identity.

Such essentialism need not be argued as scientific. Wicca already had an essentialism of sorts, since Gardner talked of the witches he met as having remembered him from past lives [Gardner 1959]. Other metaphysical explanations of what brought people to the Craft, whether in terms of past incarnations, a calling, or simply as having always felt that they were a witch, all offer the same identification with one's being a witch as

---

55 Positions on this question can be required to support some views opposed to Gay liberation: a theology that allows for Free Will can only condemn homosexuality in and of itself, as opposed to condemning only homosex, if homosexuality is a choice. Contra to this, if homosexuality is innate, then it is arguably irrational for those who already condemn racism and sexism, to not also condemn homophobia; an argument important to pre-Stonewall "homophile" organizations, and to the debate that preceded the British decriminalization of homosexuality, in 1967.

essential; that witches are born rather than made. This counters any sense that other religious minorities have a stronger link to the subcultures that develops around those religions, and a smaller element of volition in their suffering whatever oppression may exist against them, in having been born into that religion (as the majority of members of the majority of religions have), rather than having converted to it (as the majority of witches have, especially considering that with Traditional Wicca, and most forms of Innovative Witchcraft, even children raised Pagan are not brought into the Craft, unless they choose that themselves as adults). The various views that one has "always been a witch" all serve to strengthen witches' association with the identity of the witch, which then has a stronger potential influence on their politics.

Finally, since identity is defined by denomination—to name a group is to create the possibility of identifying either oneself, or another, as part of it—and since media representations will affect how people perceive each other across the boundaries of such denominations, issues concerning representation, in the press, entertainment media, and particularly in education, became increasingly important within Identity Politics. (The related, and sometimes overlapping, matter of *representation*, in the sense of having a voice on different forums, will be examined more closely in chapter 10.) Naomi Klein argues this happened to the exclusion of other concerns, writing about her own experience as a self-described "ID Warrior" during her student days, she concludes:

> Over time, campus identity politics became so consumed by personal politics that they all but eclipsed the rest of the world. The slogan "the personal is political" came to replace the

economic as political and, in the end, the political as political as well. The more importance we placed on representation issues, the more central a role they seemed to elbow for themselves in our lives.... (Klein 2001)

Such concerns were always high on the list of concerns within Wicca. Controversies about first Gardner, and later Sanders, the Frosts, and other public witches, within witchcraft were most often about the representations created by their dealings with the media. Controversies about contemporary figures still seem to focus more on concerns about how the Craft or Paganism more generally is being represented, than on the actual words and deeds that the contention arises from. Like "coming out of the closet", the phrase "coming out of the broom closet", ceased to refer just to the needs and concerns of each individual choosing to be more public about an aspect of his or her life, but also the potential implications for the entire populace of people who share that aspect.

In terms of journalism and statements claiming to be non-fictitious, the Pagan Federation's media officer, the Witches Anti-Defamation League, the Witches' League for Public Awareness and others worked an increasingly successful campaign to fight first the most blatant cases of bigotry, and later increasingly subtle statements that portrayed the Craft in a negative light. Fictitious representations were also to become an increasing concern, as they were for other groups engaging in Identity Politics. Since a particular concern of such fictitious representations, is the effect they have on young people, both within and without the groups in question, it may be worth first looking at young people engaging in witchcraft.

7.2 Teen Witches

As a priesthood, as a fertility cult that exists in a society where such religions do not inform the general culture, and as a mystery tradition, Traditional Wicca has always been a path for adults with very few exceptions. The position of younger people in Innovative Witchcraft will of course depend on how much any given practice retains those three elements, along with other concerns.

The wider Pagan community though, does not necessarily have any of these three elements, and there has always been a place for younger people, especially the children of witches and other Pagans, within it. The earliest *general* concern about young people in regards to Wicca, began with this focus on the children of Pagans. Questions about discrimination in schooling and from their peers, of isolation from other Pagan youths, given the small size of the community generally combined with the relative lack of mobility of young people, and of how, and to what extent (if at all) children should be involved in rites specifically designed to be "family orientated", were the main concerns about young people within the Pagan community, until quite recently.

As the degree of public awareness of witchcraft continued to grow (as it had been doing steadily since *Witchcraft Today*), and as with the advent of the Internet and the easy availability of books (along with an affluent period in which children typically had enough disposable income to purchase some of them) there arose an increasingly large number of teenagers with a direct interest in the Craft, or in other elements of Paganism, themselves most often not the children of Pagan parents.

The question of how to deal with such children, became a difficult question for the Pagan community. Many adult witches can relate directly; either they at least felt drawn to the Craft from

126

a young age, and in retrospect feel that they were already destined to become witches, or they themselves were actively working, or at least researching, some sort of witchcraft or other esoteric subjects. One or two may have managed to make it to covens prior to the age of majority who would accept them with their parents' permission. Many would have read about, and perhaps practised, some form of magic. Experiences of a psychic, religious, mystical, or fey nature, that brought people to their practice would often have started and been at their most intense, during childhood. Often such experiences could have led to stress, or a sense of isolation.

Such a history could lead one to sympathy with the position of young people interested in the Craft, but not necessarily to the same conclusions as to what should be done about it. Some may feel that the path that led them to the Craft was necessary, and could not have been shortened. Traditional Wicca, and many forms of Innovative Witchcraft, simply are adult-only practices, with some hesitant to train even younger adults [Guerra 2008], so even if practitioners do attempt to help children with such spiritual inclinations, then that would by necessity have to stand outside of their core practices. Others may feel that such children are best helped by themselves or by peers.

The best-known attempt by an adult practitioner to directly speak to a teenage audience, is probably Silver Ravenwolf's *Teen Witch* [Ravenwolf 1998], followed by more books and products in its wake. Where it stands in difference to other introductions to witchcraft, including previous works by the same author, as far as witchcraft itself is concerned, is hard to say. There is an attempt to create a young person's version of an existing text, but the text in question, the statement by the American Council of Witches

[CAW 1974], is neither difficult in the original, directly educational (being a terse document intended to explain witchcraft to cowans, rather than holding any liturgical, ritual or Craft purpose), nor of relevance to any witches other than those who may happen to decide they agree with it. One rewording in particular, stands as an extremely dubious interpretation:

> 11. As American Witches, we are not threatened by debates on the history of the Craft, the origins of various terms, the origins of various aspects of different traditions. We are concerned with our present and our future.

Teen speak:
> There is no one right way to practice the Craft. The religion is what you make of it.

Apart from this, there are attempts to address concerns that teenagers may have in their lives, but they seem primarily to be an attempt to address the concerns that teenagers are somehow *supposed* to have; bullying, an extremely asymmetric form of heterosexual teenage romance, grades, and difficulties with teachers. More difficult problems are wrapped up with the "just say no" message that roundly failed to make any impact on drug-use by minors in the late 1980s, and a general suggestion that one should talk to responsible adults about serious problems, but without any attempt to address the difficulty teenagers, or indeed adults, may find in actually doing so. In all, it's difficult to see this as any attempt to assist any teenagers with an interest in the Craft, but rather as an exercise in market diversification, of the sort that Klein argues absorbed Identity Politics into commercial concerns.

128

The view on the basic concept among adult witches is unfortunately made difficult to judge by criticism about the contents of the book, particularly in terms of the ethics of using what she describes as "a double sneak attack" to lie to one's parents, the puritan and sexist sexual morality, and a repeat of the criticisms often levelled at her earlier books. The author seems to have deliberately attempted to present such criticism as a lack of support for the concerns of teenagers—"you may not care about teens but I do"—leading to an even greater polarization of opinion. The success of this polarizing tactic makes it hard to find critiques that do not either support the book full-heartedly, or which do not handle the more general question of how the question of teen witches should be handled (if at all) in criticism of other aspects of the book. The fact that many criticizing the book are themselves teenagers, offers that this is merely a book aimed at them that doesn't succeed in its objectives, but leaves the wider question still open; could there be a *Teen Witch* that met with greater enthusiasm from other witches? What would such a book, if indeed a book would be the best medium, be like? This would seem to be still unanswered.

Similarly, Oberon Zell's "Grey School of Wizardry", [Greyschool] an online course in magic which accepts both minors and adults, will inevitably provoke the same criticism that is made about other online courses, such as that run by "Witch School" [Witchschool], along with courting disfavour from many, in its borrowing various items of terminology from the *Harry Potter* series.[56] There is too much controversy as to how it attempts to

---

56   In fairness, if anyone could build something found to be of real spiritual or magical significance from Harry Potter, it would be Zell with his success in having done so with Heinlein's *Stranger in a Strange Land*.

teach children to judge the balance of opinions on doing so in the first place.

The least controversial, though by no means entirely controversy-free, attempts to engage with younger people interested in the Craft, have been those which have given them a voice themselves. The Pagan Federation's "Minor Arcana" and the youth section of Witchvox.com, are both successful, at least as measured by the level of interest they have received from members of their target demographic. With the influence of adults being less direct, and less autocratic, and hence with less risk of "power over" [Starhawk 1979] that makes many Pagans suspicious wherever it arises, it would seem that this is the model that support networks for younger Pagans and witches will be built on in the future. That same degree of independence means that support for its membership from older Pagans may be less available, particularly as the organizing capabilities of the Internet may lead to the next generation of support networks existing without any adult involvement at all. If this is the case, then perhaps the potential problems are no more answered than they were before.

7.3 Bubblegum for the Eyes

The interest in witchcraft among teenagers has been frequently associated by commentators, whether within witchcraft, the Christian Right, or the mainstream media, with popular culture portrayals of witchcraft. As seen previously, there is also an interest in such popular culture representations, stemming from the importance placed on such by Identity Politics. This in turn often turns back to issues concerning youth, due to the fact that most popular culture representations of witchcraft are either in

130

shows and books aimed specifically at youths, or with a large youth audience, and that often the fictional witches of these portrayals are themselves youths.

Earlier representations of youths involved in witchcraft have deliberately contrasted the common representations of witches as inherently evil (such as "The Wicked Witch of the West"), or inherently wise (such as "The Good Witch of the North"), with the acceptable view of teenagers and children as basically good, but inherently given to folly, as in Harvey Comics' *Wendy the Good Little Witch* (1954), and Archie Comics' *Sabrina the Teenage Witch* (1962). This trope would probably reach its largest audience with the television series *Bewitched* [Saks 1964], which this time contrasted the conventional stereotype of a "devoted" housewife, with the mischief apparently inherent to its concept of the witch, while likewise contrasting the power of such witches with a paternalistic view of women. While commonly said to be based on *I Married a Witch* [Clair 1942], or *Bell, Book and Candle* [Quine 1958], the ongoing episodic format doesn't allow the contrasting views of natural and supernatural women to be resolved, as they are in those movies, and so its portrayal of witchcraft, and how it interacts with the mundane world, is closer to *Sabrina* and *Wendy*, than to any other contemporary popular culture representations.

One particularly noteworthy feature of all these representations, is that witches are ontologically different to humans (referred to as "mortals" in both *Bewitched* and *Sabrina*). They are a different species, and are immigrants to our world from planes inaccessible to humanity. As such they are even further removed from reality than vampires, werewolves, and ghosts; the more prevalent stock characters of both horror and horror-comedy. Hence, they offer very little in way of inspiration, or analogy to

131

any real form of witchcraft, beyond tongue-in-cheek references. Even Jack Chick, normally prepared to accuse just about anything of being part of a massive Catholic-Masonic-Satanic-Pagan-Jewish conspiracy, seems to blame *Bewitched* only for culturally opening the doors for later media representations [Chick 2000].

Popular culture references to witchcraft and Paganism largely remained entirely distinct from reality, with *The Wicker Man* [Hardy 1973] standing as an exception in its degree of mundane plausibility; requiring an extraordinary conspiracy, but not any impossible fantastic elements.

This exception aside, any concept of witchcraft as existing in the real world was at most one-off, tongue-in-cheek episodes of shows like *Knight Rider* [Kolbe 1984], often Hallowe'en specials, which would hint at a witchcraft as existing in the "real" world, or at the efficacy of magic, or both, but do no more than hint.

Towards the end of the eighties, fictional use of witches would be responded to increasingly by organized protests such as those by the Witches' League for Public Awareness demanding that the movie of *The Witches of Eastwick* [Miller 1987] have a disclaimer distancing its portrayals from real witches similar to a disclaimer distancing the *Godfather* trilogy from Italian-Americans [Cabot 1992].

By the end of the 1990s, there were four different changes in the portrayal of witchcraft in popular fiction.

The first change is that shows such as *The X-Files*, in using common fictional tropes concerning witchcraft, magic, or Satanism, would explicitly distance the storyline from Wicca [Manners 1995]. Concerns about perceptions of "Political Correctness" in light of such protests as those about *Eastwick*, and

132

perhaps awareness of the relatively large number of Pagans amongst science-fiction's audience, could only allow such storylines if they are clearly differentiated from Wicca, either through characters pointedly making statements about the Rede, or describing Wicca as "peaceful", or through the plot eventually showing any characters identified as witches to be innocent of any wrong-doing, or indeed responsible for some heroism. Even *Scooby-Doo* has differentiated Wiccan "eco-goths" from fairy tale witches [Strenstrum 1999 & Jeralds 2003], along with associating the accused witches of the American colonies with the former.

The second change was an increased number of plot lines identifying Wicca as a religion whose members' rights deserve protection by the (usually American) state, often in legal dramas such as *Judging Amy* [Karon 1999].

The third and fourth changes interact with each other deeply. Simultaneously, there was increasing influence of artefacts and terminology of Wiccan practice present in the successors to *Sabrina* (including the televised version of the same) and *Bewitched*, along with an expressed view from just about all quarters, that these were encouraging teenagers to develop an interest in witchcraft, a view that few would argue was held about *Bewitched*.

These two cannot be easily separated, as they feed into each other. Sony Pictures' *The Craft* [Fleming 1996] was controversial within the Pagan community since before shooting was finished, for taking inspiration from actual practice, and at this point even the technical advisor from Covenant of the Goddess seemed to feel it would influence some young people into copycat acts, given her feeling that using a fictional god-name would prevent, "hordes of teenagers running down to the beach or out to the

133

woods invoking anybody real" [COG 1995]. Indeed she seems to feel that ultimately this is a positive thing:

> As you know, Ethical Witches do not proselytize. *The Craft* was seen by approximately one million people in its first weekend. If one in ten of those people are intrigued enough to look into the subject further, maybe read a book (and now there are shelves full of books!) that's 100,000 people who will at least be more educated about our reality. If one in ten of those people chose to pursue the subject further, that's 10,000 people out of the first weekend.

What is not stated is just where the line lies between proselytizing and convincing 1% of an audience, who had expressed no prior interest in practising any form of witchcraft, to do so.

In the end, *The Craft* had only a modest box-office impact [Box Office Mojo], and seems to be better-known as a theoretical reason for attracting "fluffy" people to witchcraft, than it is outside of this. Perhaps what is really needed, is not anything to debunk the idea that witches regularly change their eyes' colour magically, but rather to debunk the idea that many people believe that they do.

While outside of the Pagan community, *The Craft* passed by largely unnoticed, much more attention was paid to TV series *Sabrina the Teenage Witch* [Scovell 1996], *Buffy the Vampire Slayer* [Whedon 1997], and *Charmed* [Burges 1998], and increasingly the books [Rowling 1997], and later the films [Columbus 2001], of the *Harry Potter* series.

Like the comic book series on which *Sabrina* was based, the witches in *Sabrina* are not entirely human. Similarly, in *Charmed*, witchcraft is entirely essential, and inherited, and while the

134

differentiation between "mortal" humans and witches is not as extreme as in *Sabrina* and *Bewitched*, it is closer to that than to anything else. Likewise, *Harry Potter* posits witchcraft as essential (even explicitly mirroring racial discrimination in how some characters behave), to a much greater degree than it is learned, and the degree to which it reflects any real views of magic drops sharply, from the first book mentioning such historical figures as Nicolas Flamel, and various items of occult trivia [Rowling 1997], to quickly become much more self-contained.

Charmed does however make use of some terminology that is associated with Wicca, but not generally part of earlier fictional concepts of witchcraft. In particular the word *Wicca* itself is used; infrequently but prominently, such as the title of the pilot episode, "Something Wicca This Way Comes" [Kretchmer 1998], along with the expressions "Book of Shadows" and "Blessed Be".

As such, there would definitely appear to be an element of dialogue between *Charmed* and the wider Wiccan and Pagan community, albeit a largely unbalanced one. *Charmed* grabs some low-hanging linguistic fruit from the community, while many in the community express irritation with the wider Western society, in how it portrays them, and largely wish to distance themselves from it, even (especially?) if they end up caught up in the storyline.

Buffy the Vampire Slayer is a significantly more complicated case though. At first glance, it seems to also be looking to Wicca solely for the same sort of verbal source material as does *Charmed*. However, a richer relationship between the witchcraft of *Buffy's* diegesis and Wicca quickly emerges, and this increased as the series progressed, as the main Wiccan character, Willow

135

Rosenberg, learns more about witchcraft, and as the writers solidified how witchcraft is constructed within the show.

A first item of significance, is that unlike the majority of such television programs, Willow Rosenberg is not ontologically different to anybody else; she is not a superhero, unlike the series' eponymous character, or a different manner of being to any other human, but rather her witchcraft is something she learns. While her talent eventually makes her comparable with the most powerful supernatural characters on the show, she is a Mozart or a Shakespeare, not a Kal-El or Peter Parker. The potential as an inspiration to a viewer is perhaps accordingly different to that of *Sabrina* or *Charmed*.

The biggest difference is how magic is portrayed in the show. For the most part, a variety of different clichés of fictional magic are used, from the extreme ease of merely needing to know the correct "magic words" (self-satirized when a character causes a fire by reading *"librum incendere"* aloud and is chided "Don't speak Latin in front of the books" [Espenson 2000]) or the infeasibly rare object (self-satirized in the series' spin-off, when a character fails to obtain a box "handcrafted by blind Tibetan monks", and substitutes one "pieced together by mute Chinese nuns" [Renshaw 2000]). The series' own satire of these clichés demonstrates an awareness of the absurdity they can often reach. Much of Willow's magic though, becomes increasingly visceral and "natural" as the storyline develops. Apart from offering better assistance to the audiences suspension of disbelief, the nature of Willow's relationship with magic grows in some important ways.

First, her identity increasingly becomes that of a witch. The character is introduced as a bookish form of the classic "rebel without a cause". She is privileged in education, wealth (while not rich, she is from a comfortable middle-class background, and generally the one to purchase any needed equipment), and ethnicity (while nominally Jewish, this is something we are rarely told and never shown; she is firmly assimilated), yet fails to fit in or to access or acknowledge the benefits of her privilege. She is constantly at odds with the authorities of her privilege, and her academic success is more often despite, rather than because of her educators. Her relatively privileged position manifests primarily as guilt about such concerns as indigenous rights [Espenson 1999]. As such, she is at war with her own identity, and the identity of a witch allows her to develop her own sense of herself, especially as it comes in conjunction with her identifying as lesbian (or perhaps more accurately, as bisexual). While I've argued above that she differs from such fictional witches as Sabrina, in not being inherently different from the fictional cowans of the story, her expressed *self-image* is essentialist, akin to that currently popular in terms of queer identity, and her identity as a witch, as well as that as a lesbian, are both akin to that of many gay, lesbian and bisexual people at the turn of the century.

The connection between her use of magic and her sexuality becomes increasingly pronounced. Both she and her girlfriend will refer to plans to "experiment" with magic with a clear subtext, both between the characters, and to the audience, that they are also planning sexual experimentation, and their responses performing magic are visually ecstatic, nearly orgasmic [Whedon 2000a]. Increasingly, the identity of the two as witches and lesbians becomes conflated to the point of being one and the same. Yet this is prevented from allowing one to become a mere cipher for the other, by existing in a storyline where there are

137

other magic workers, along with enough self-satire of this conflation to build up audience resistance to it. Lesbian sexuality is not being conflated with witchcraft by the show itself, but rather that conflation is a personal response made by the character, and her peers, in her search for identity. Again, like the degree of essentialism that she seems to feel exists in her identity as a witch, it is the characters themselves which combine those two identities, not the series' writers.

It is also worth noting, that while the portrayal of a homosexual relationship garnered much commentary, both positive and negative, at the time, it is arguably the most normal relationship in the entire series; both parties are fully human, the relationship is moderately and quietly kinky but without overt signs of such kinks causing distress,[57] there is little tension around gender roles, and while it ends in an act of violence, both the means and the circumstance—her girlfriend is killed by a stray bullet—makes it the sort of random meaningless horror that can enter into any of our lives, rather than the fantastic impossibilities that are the mainstay of the programme. All of which make it unique in the series. Finally, her subsequent relationship is the only one to make it to the end of the series intact, with a chance for as close to "happily ever after" as one may hope for.

So witchcraft here is conflated with sex, but rather than doing so entirely in the sensationalist manner already common in fiction and reportage, it is conflated with expressly healthy sex compared with most other relationships portrayed in the series—with what

---

57   In a fiction that holds normalcy and claims to normalcy as suspect, in both text and subtext, yet also uses more explicit elements of kink to reflect dysfunction in relationships, this could be read as a balanced ideal.

young adults would not only hope for, but arguably *should* hope for.

At the same time, Pagan religious elements increasingly move into both the magic performed (with gods from the Egyptian and Hellenic pantheons being petitioned, but also Aradia [Fury 1999]), and her everyday thought (as reflected by using "goddess" in exclamations). Religious views aren't explored beyond such artefacts, but this holds true for the series' portrayal of religion generally, where crucifixes abound but worship does not.

Operative witchcraft, Paganism and lesbian sexuality, finally come together in a dream sequence [Whedon 2000b] where she is painting Sappho's first fragment, a petition to Aphrodite,[58] on her lover's back. At this point, we have a fictional Wicca that is religious as well as magical, differentiating it from almost all supernatural portrayals of witchcraft in previous mainstream popular culture, being conflated with as close to a romantic and sexual ideal as the series can allow.

There is however a negative side, as is required by a drama, which in this case manifests itself in first an "addiction" to magic, and finally a complete loss of her moral compass in the face of grief.

The former could be read as an analogy to drug addiction, or a reflection of the concern parents will have for adolescents and young adults engaging in any sexual activity, no matter how healthy. Increasingly though, the reading most directly offered is that rather than find authenticity, she has lost herself in her new identity, which is suggested by the finale, where she regains her

---

58 "Ποικιλόθρον', ἀθανάτ' Ἀφρόδιτα, παῖ Δίος..."; "Immortal Aphrodite of the broidered throne, daughter of Zeus..." (Wharton's translation, see www.classicpersuasion.org/pw/sappho/sape01u.htm).

sense of moral proportion by being reminded not just of this identity, but of how she was as a child in kindergarten [Fury 2002].

Where Identity Politics has led to demands for positive media representation, *Buffy* has responded not merely with characters that are non-heteronormative witches, but by placing such politicized identities into the questioning of identity that befits its wider theme of adolescence, and going on to problematize the investment of too much psychic energy into such identities. It doesn't merely respond to the demands of Identity Politics, but engages them head-on.

While these particular fictions have made the most impact in terms of how much they are perceived to be influencing young people to develop an interest in witchcraft, a large part of this is simply that they are relatively successful and well-known examples of what young people are watching, or are expected to watch. This notoriety owes as much to the fact that they are popular enough with an older audience to be known to them, and they are relatively mainstream, than anything else.

Less popular books and comics with magical themes often hold a small but deeply loyal following. Laurel K. Hamilton's *Anita Blake* series beginning with *Guilty Pleasures* [Hamilton 2002], describes magic as deriving from a sort of energy that comes from the protagonist's body. While she quickly moves away from this into more fantastic descriptions, these most basic descriptions of magic are not far removed from what is found in Gardner. The lack of restrictions on her medium also allows her to mix her descriptions of magic with a much more explicit combination of violence, sexual identity and kink, than Whedon could in *Buffy*, so we should expect it to garner more controversy. Neil Gaiman's comic-book epic *The Sandman*, while one of the best known comic-book series in the English language, is still somewhat outside of the mainstream, even as he himself has broken into it with other media. He has quite explicitly played on the assumption that he would have a large Wiccan and Pagan audience, basing a plot-point on the expectation that he could shock readers who were familiar with Wiccan concepts of Drawing Down the Moon, but not the earlier belief that Thessalian witches could physically take the moon from its orbit [Bender 2000]. Conversely, while his later novel, *American Gods* [Gaiman 2001], garnered more mainstream acclaim while dealing explicitly with a variety of pantheons which are honoured within modern Paganism, it is a large volume with a clear adult audience, and the fact that a large number of teenagers have undoubtedly read it, is pretty much ignored.

Beyond general suspicion of comic books and horror fiction in many quarters, and a general suspicion of almost all media within some elements of the Christian Right, these are rarely mentioned as possible influencers of teenage witches. Yet if any of the regular suspects actually do have such an effect, then these should be at least as likely to have as strong, if not a stronger, effect upon their readers. While audience-size is in itself a reason to focus one's attention in particular directions, the irrationally reactive nature of the scaremongering suggests a moral panic, rather than any realistic assessment. This is all the more evident when we consider that Gaiman and Hamilton are both best-selling authors and by any objective standard their audience is large, suggesting that it is purely the greater media hype that surrounded *Buffy* and *Harry Potter* that has triggered the concerns about their effect upon their audience.

Similarly, the lack of concern about more respectable novels, if we can take critical acclaim in broadsheets as a measure of such, reflects a degree of snobbery about popular culture. This would probably not apply to those who see witchcraft as inherently evil, but could affect how seriously teenagers are taken by older witches.

Chapter Eight

National and Tribal Cultures as Source Text

"First they came to take our land and water, then our fish and game. Then they wanted our mineral resources and, to get them, they tried to take our governments. Now they want our religions as well."
—Janet McCloud, *Z Magazine*, December 1990.

Building on the work of the Farrars in identifying influences upon Gardner [Farrar & Farrar 1981 and Farrar & Farrar 1984], Hutton has demonstrated that many elements of Traditional Wicca relate to cultural events in the eighteenth, nineteenth and early twentieth centuries [Hutton 1999]. He largely left open the question of what influences from before that period were at work, though has certainly leant more support to sceptical positions on the question, whether that was his intent or not.

Almost all of the sources are among those to which Gardner could, either as a Briton or as a European, make some degree of claim. Similarly, when the Farrars gave an exposition of the manner in which they introduced local (that is, Irish) elements into their Sabbat celebrations [Farrar & Farrar 1981], they were doing so as residents of Ireland, and as such as people with a claim to the experience they drew on.

Many people feel drawn towards a culture that they cannot make such a direct claim on. Many other such claims are made on different grounds to others making the same claim. Consider that a US-born US citizen with Irish ancestors may feel "Irish", though he not only does not have the same claims as an Irish-born Irish citizen, but further that the claims he does have are not shared by all Irish citizens (who may be naturalized citizens born elsewhere). Other people feel drawn towards a variety of cultures, or just towards a variety of artefacts of different cultures.

It is notable that Traditional Wiccans will often also work with gods from a variety of cultures, as well as those of the Wicca, and have often explained aspects of their Craft in terms of practices from around the world (especially, but not exclusively, from Europe), whether claiming they are doing the same, or merely drawing analogy. It is also notable that some have agreed with, or at least paid some respect to, the soft polytheism of Dion Fortune,[59] and earlier Neoplatonic combinations of monotheism and polytheism, with the justification for extreme levels of syncretism these imply. Finally, often analogies to other cultures offers a mechanism by which one can talk about aspects of Traditional Wicca, while staying clear from matters that they may feel it would impinge upon their oaths to raise more directly.

Innovative Witchcraft inherits much of this, but often not as much of the original cultural background of Traditional Wicca, especially for practitioners outside of England, and more so outside of Western Europe. Often within these practices what is considered Wicca is taken to be a framework, around which cultural borrowings can be attached, producing a practice that would then be labelled, *Irish Wicca*, *Pictish Wicca*, *Norse Wicca*, or in

---

59 "All gods are one God, all goddesses are one Goddess, and there is one Initiator." [Fortune 1938].

the case of more deeply syncretistic practices, *Eclectic Wicca*.[60] The tendency for syncretism in the New Age Movement would be another influence, encouraging this latter eclectic use of cultural borrowings from a variety of cultures, though by the same token, the disdain for the New Age Movement that is common within much modern Paganism, particularly in the wake of the anti-fluffy backlash, serves as a disincentive with growing impact.

That one not only can, but should, combine Wiccan-derived techniques with such cultural borrowings, is so commonly stated as to be part of the loose orthodoxy I have suggested has emerged within Innovative Witchcraft. In introductory books, it is often suggested that deciding upon which culture, or cultures, to borrow from, is the first step in developing a practice. This decision is a key factor in what is seen to define a particular Innovative Tradition [Grimassi 2008].

With a variety of cultures being so used, there is hence a desire for information not only on Wicca, and on the cultures in question, but on how any particular culture may be combined with Wicca. This creates an automatic market diversification, which perhaps could lead publishers to favour this approach to magic and religion, and has certainly led to criticism that such practice treats cultures as little more than consumer choices. Certainly the similarity between the two following citations from D. J. Conway, the first pertaining to explain Celtic magic, the second Norse, seems to indicate no difference more profound than branding:

---

60 As noted in the first chapter, *Eclectic* is often used within Traditional Wicca to describe all Innovative Witchcraft. The disparity between that use, and how it is used within Innovative Witchcraft, being my reason for coining the latter term.

Carry the burner around the circle clockwise, beginning in the east. Return it to the altar.

Go to the eastern quarter of the circle. Light the red (yellow) candle[61] and hold your hand up in greeting. You may also salute the Element with your dagger, sword or wand instead of your hand:

> I call upon you, Powers of Air, to witness this rite and to guard this circle.

In the southern quarter, light the white (red) candle and greet the Element:

> I call upon you, Powers of Fire, to witness this rite and to guard this circle.

Move to the west; light the grey (blue) candle and hold your hand in greeting:

> I call upon you, Powers of Water, to witness this rite and to guard this circle.

End by going to the north; light the black (green) candle and greet the Element:

> I call upon you, Powers of Earth, to witness this rite and to guard this circle.

Carry the burner around the circle clockwise, beginning in the east. Return it to the altar.

Go to the eastern quarter of the circle. Light the yellow candle and hold your hand up in greeting. You may also salute the Element with your dagger, sword or wand instead of your hand:

> I call upon you, Powers of Air, to witness this rite and to guard this circle.

Move to the south; light the red candle and greet the Element:

> I call upon you, Powers of Fire, to witness this rite and to guard this circle.

In the western quarter you light the blue candle and hold your hand in greeting:

> I call upon you, Powers of Water, to witness this rite and to guard this circle.

End by going to the north; light the green candle and greet the Element:

> I call upon you, Powers of Earth, to witness this rite and to guard this circle.

---

61 Earlier in this text she had described associations between colours and directions in which yellow, red, blue, and dark green (deosil, starting from the East) were "Wiccan" and red, white, grey, and black were "Celtic."

Move back to the central altar, and stand facing east. Raise your arms in greeting:

This circle is bound,
With power all around.
Between the worlds, I stand
With protection at hand.

Proceed with your planned spellworking or ceremony. When everything is completed, hold you hand or dagger over the altar and say:

By the powers of the ancient Gods,
I bind all power within this circle
Into this spell. So mote it be.

When you are ready to end the ritual, go to the east and extinguish the red (yellow) candle. Say:

Depart in peace, O Powers of Air.
My thanks and blessings.

Go to the south, extinguish the white (red) candle. Say:

Depart in peace, O Powers of Fire.
My thanks and blessings.

Go to the west and put out the grey (blue) candle. Say:

Depart in peace, O Powers of
Water.
My thanks and blessings.

Move back to the central altar, and stand facing east. Raise your arms in greeting:

This circle is bound,
With power all around.
Within it I stand
With protection at hand.

Proceed with your planned spellworking or ceremony. When everything is completed, hold you hand or ritual tool over the altar and say:

By the powers of the ancient Gods,
I bind all power within this circle
Into this spell. So mote it be!

When you are ready to end the ritual, go to the east and extinguish the yellow candle. Say:

Depart in peace, O Powers of Air.
My thanks and blessings.

Go to the south, extinguish the red candle. Say:

Depart in peace, O Powers of Fire.
My thanks and blessings.

Go to the west and put out the blue candle. Say:

Depart in peace, O Powers of
Water.
My thanks and blessings.

Finish by going to the north and extinguishing the black (green) candle. Say:

Depart in peace, O Powers of
   Earth.
My thanks and blessings.

Return to the altar in the center and say:

To all beings and powers of the
   visible and invisible, depart in
   peace.
May there always be harmony
   between us.
My thanks and blessings.

Cut the circle with a backwards movement of your dagger or sword to release all remaining traces of power for manifestation. Say:

The circle is open, yet ever it
   remains a circle.
Around and through me always
   flows its magical power.

Put away all magical tools and clear the altar. Leave any candles or object which must remain either to burn out or be empowered for a stated period of time.

You have completed a ritual. Practice will make the power flow easier and more freely. You will become more self-confident. Soon you will be looking forward to the time you spend between the worlds with the Ancient Ones. [Conway 1990a]

Finish by going to the north and extinguishing the green candle. Say:

Depart in peace, O Powers of
   Earth.
My thanks and blessings.

Return to the center to stand before the altar. Raise your arms and say:

To all beings and powers of the
   visible and invisible, depart in
   peace.
May there always be harmony
   between us.
My thanks and blessings.

Cut the circle with a backwards movement of your dagger or sword to release all remaining traces of power for manifestation. Say:

The circle is open, yet ever it
   remains a circle.
Around and through me always
   flows its magical power.

Put away all magical tools and clear the altar. Leave any candles or object which must remain either to burn out or be empowered for a stated period of time.

You have completed a ritual. Practice will make the power flow easier and more freely. You will become more self-confident. Soon you will be looking forward to ritual and spellworking. [Conway 1990b]

This could be viewed as a cynical exercise on Conway's part, but it is also quite possible that she genuinely views culture in this way, and considers this to be completely valid and useful, and to truly reflect something of the culture in each book's title.

Those with different attachments to the culture in question may see things differently. One major point of criticism is that the cultural and historical material presented is often of questionable accuracy to begin with. Joanna Hautin-Mayer's critique "When is a Celt not a Celt?" [Hautin-Mayer] examines six works examining Celtic history and culture in different ways, and her verdict of four of them condemns them sharply. Of these four, all could be considered to be Neopagan in some manner, and two of them, *Witta* [McCoy 1993], and *Faery Wicca* [Stepanich 1994 & Stepanich 1998], describe forms of post-Gardnerian witchcraft. Hautin-Mayer's critique pretty firmly established that these books were of little value in terms of what they portrayed themselves as providing. The essay, being widely circulated, helped fuel several debates, not just about cultural borrowing, but the state of scholarship in Pagan publications, the value of syncretism generally, the anti-fluffy backlash, and the general quality of works published by Llewellyn Worldwide (which published both those volumes, and some of the others Hautin-Mayer examined).

Within Neopaganism, the strongest criticisms tend to come from reconstructionist religions, like Celtic Reconstructionism and Hellenicism. Since cultures which have continued into the current age, particularly the cultures indigenous to the Americas, have also been used in this manner, and given that the people belonging to these cultures have often experienced very severe oppression from people of the white Anglo ethnicity from which Wicca came, that continues to this day, much of the harshest criticism has been from those quarters. Other cultures that have not received as much attention from Innovative Witches are often of interest to the New Age Movement, which makes this interest likely to cross along the overlap between the New Age Movement and Innovative Witchcraft in the near future.

The more extreme cases of "plastic shamans", whose statements can be demonstrated to be factually incorrect in much the same the manner that Hautin-Mayer did with *Witta* and *Faery Wicca* are one thing. More contentious are arguments that indigenous cultures, or at least certain aspects of them, should not be used in this manner at all.

Between these two complaints, lies that which argues that the form of adoption of such cultural elements is not wrong in itself, but not possible within the frameworks that they are being used in: All of the New Age Moment, and much of Innovative Witchcraft, places a high regard on personal development, to the extent that this is seen as the very point of such practice. (Though Traditional Wiccans may speak of the personally transformative effects that working Wicca can bring about [Crowley 1989b], Traditional Wicca, and much of the rest of Innovative Witchcraft, does not place such personal development in the position of a goal in itself.) The larger religions with global reach also contain elements of personal importance, in regards to their own concepts of Salvation (Christianity), or Enlightenment (Buddhism). While such traditions as vision quests are promoted as similarly of personal benefit to the participant, originally "the context was a belief that the person's individual life and calling was a gift for the whole group, and their connection to the spirit world would bring them into deeper connection with the community, bringing life to the community" [Johnson 1995]. Here, the criticism does not

150

necessarily go so far as to criticize all borrowings, nor complain that the borrowing is necessarily inaccurate, but rather that the context it has been borrowed into brings inaccuracies and disrespect for the original.

A final stream of criticism rests upon the degree of effort taken to approach the culture in question on its terms. Lora O'Brien's advice to those with an interest in Irish forms of witchcraft, starts with suggesting that people learn at least the modern form of the Irish language [O'Brien 2004]. While she does not insist that this would be absolutely necessary, the difference in the degree of effort required, and the level of understanding of the culture that any practice would then be rooted in, stands in stark contrast to the works mentioned so far.

The debates on this matter will probably never be resolved. The motives of those involved on both sides can be earnest, apart from the more extreme cases of fraud. There is no absolute means by which cultural boundaries can be drawn to allow for any absolute resolution, unless extreme forms of segregation become the norm, leading to members of some cultures viewing as "theirs" what members of another see as having been appropriated, including from one indigenous tribe to another, such as the Hopi have accused the Navajo of doing [Brown 2003b].

It is hard to imagine Italian cuisine today existing without tomatoes or pasta, though the use of both as foods are cultural borrowings, from the Americas and the Middle East, with the latter in turn being an Arab borrowing from further East. While such simple borrowings may seem trivial and obvious (one doesn't often care much about the ethnobotany of one's ragù, though the ethnobotany of potentially patentable medicines is a much more contentious issue [Brown 2003b]), the lines of "trivial" and "obvious" can be difficult to draw, since such matters as culinary use of plants and other technological developments with obvious advantages (especially to people now sharing the environment in which they developed), can be of great cultural significance. Indeed, borrowings can develop great cultural significance in the cultures into which they were borrowed. The national and regional cuisines, for example, of Europe are more heavily defined by differences in adoptions from the New World, than any earlier distinctions. While claims that potatoes were used in ancient Irish rites is one of the grounds on which Hautin-Mayer criticized both *Witta* and *Faery Wicca*, the fact remains that it has been a staple of the Irish diet for centuries; more than long enough to establish a place in the *modern* culture, as well as the diet, not least in the wake of the Great Hunger of the 1840s. Similarly cultures are not static; colcannon may be attested no earlier than late eighteenth century [Brewer 1899], which makes claims of it being used for divination in ancient times infeasible, but its use in a divination game, albeit one not taken very seriously,[62] is certainly an Irish tradition today.

Such a place for a South American crop in Irish culture stands at a considerable distance from claims to be able to represent a spiritual inheritance from either Ireland or the Americas, but as long as there are nits to pick, they will be picked. Are moccasins part of Native American culture (and if so, which tribes), or are they merely a comfortable way to make shoes from soft leather? Is wearing them to a powwow different to wearing them to the

---

62 Any man growing up with the tradition will have had a life as a "spinster" foretold at some point, and any woman a life as a "bachelor", along with a life of both poverty and riches, so neither are likely to pay it much heed.

office? If borrowing moccasins is okay, then is it okay to borrow dream-catchers if your culture lacks any alternative metaphysical technology for preventing bad dreams? If dream-catchers are okay, then why not medicine drums? If one determines that use of sweat lodges outside of their American context crosses the line, what of looking to them for possible insight into what may have been once part of the Northern European use of sweating, such as evolved into the saunas of Scandinavia? And if that is acceptable, precisely how can such insights be used without insult to either culture?

Michael F. Brown discusses approaches based on adapting existing concepts of Intellectual Property to better deal with such issues [Brown 2003b], but notes many potential problems which suggest that such an approach could perhaps cause more harm than good, even if one can successfully fit different cultural ideas of ownership into such a model. One immediate problem with an IP-based approach, is that such Intellectual Property cannot be defended unless it is identified. To keep the details of ceremonies and religious practice secret remains the best guarantee that such practices are not used in ways the originating community would not approve, but to do so means that false claims cannot be easily refuted, and leaks are harder to deal with after the fact. Brown also notes that Lawrence Lessig and others have criticized the extent of existing Intellectual Property laws, as most use of information is "nonrivalrous"; my use of Einstein's Theory of Relativity does not deplete your ability to use it too. Given that such opposition to current concepts of Intellectual Property is common among young people with liberal views today, it is likely that many people that will be forming the Innovative practices of the near-future, would see such an approach analogously to media corporations that they view as stymieing their own culture, through copyright and patent laws. Certainly the rhetoric that Intellectual Property should be shared has been borrowed into defences of the most controversial marketers of Native American spirituality [Red Road 1993]. However, some in the hacker subculture, probably the group most strongly at odds with existing Intellectual Property practices, have come to view their own approach to informational resources as based on innate concepts of ownership [Raymond 2001], an insight which may reduce the degree of absolutism in any such position.

These issues will continue to affect both Traditional and Innovative practices. As well as their importance in themselves, they provide strong rhetorical ammunition to the anti-fluffy backlash, that if nothing else will make raising these issues an easy means of scoring points. Unease about the ethics of borrowing from cultures other than one's own, especially living cultures, may narrow the cultural sources that are frequently used by many witches. Meanwhile, those Traditional Wiccans who are critical of Innovative Witchcraft may find parallels between their experience of having their practice used as the basis for an identically-named practice they consider foreign, and the experiences of these cultures; even viewing the very existence of post-Gardnerian witchcraft outside of Traditional practice to in itself be a form of cultural appropriation.

Chapter Nine

Sex and Sexual Politics

"Physics is like sex. Sure, it may give some practical results, but
that's not why we do it"

—Richard Feynman.

As a fertility cult, Traditional Wicca makes use of symbolism of
sexuality as a generative force. Most obviously in the Great Rite
and the blessing of cakes and ale, though also in its use of
male–female polarity in ritual interactions, the blessing of
generative organs during the Five-Fold Kiss, and the use of a kiss
as a salute.

Every one of these aspects has made it into some Innovative
Witchcraft practice, but all have been omitted or altered in some
as well.

Anything which requires a male–female polarity is obviously
going to be dropped by single-sex groups, such as those Dianic
witches which work in female-only groups. The Traditional
male–female creative polarity has also been seen by some as
homophobic.

In defining the terms Palaeopaganism, Mesopaganism and
Neopaganism, Isaac Bonewits [1979] includes:

Some Paleopagan belief systems may be racist, sexist, homophobic, etc....

> Examples of Mesopagan belief systems would include… most orthodox (aka "British Traditionalist") denominations of Wicca.…
>
> Some Mesopagan belief systems may be racist, sexist, homophobic, etc.…
>
> Neopagan belief systems are *not* [emphasis his] racist, sexist, homophobic, etc.… Examples of Neopaganism would include… most heterodox Wiccan traditions,…

It is notable in itself that "most orthodox (aka 'British Traditionalist') denominations of Wicca" are categorized so differently to "most heterodox Wiccan traditions" since this presumably corresponds closely with the distinction between what I label *Traditional Wicca* and *Innovative Witchcraft* here.

Bonewits' inclusion of the claim that Palaeopaganism and Mesopaganism "may be racist, sexist, homophobic, etc." would seem to mainly be to contrast it with Neopaganism; "are not" could be a definition, "may be" at most an observation. The wording is hence not very conclusive as far as Traditional Wicca goes; it could after all be just as non-homophobic as he claims Neopagan Witchcraft is, while still belonging to a category that contained other religions that "may be… homophobic". But, it is quite emphatic when it comes to the Neopagan category, in which he includes "most heterodox Wiccan traditions."

While this probably is not intended to imply that nobody who identifies as Neopagan could ever be homophobic (or for that matter racist),[63] it does still strongly suggest that a lack of such discriminatory views is not just common in Neopaganism, but typical of it. Even if significant degrees of homophobia were to be

---

63 If it is, I can sadly attest that he is wrong on both counts, from the example of some Neopagans I have met.

found in Neopaganism, whether explicit in a tradition or merely found among individual practitioners, such a statement by a well-known Neopagan stands, at the very least, as a firm statement of what he thinks Neopaganism *ought to* be, and therefore we should expect to find a similar view expressed throughout Neopaganism.

Returning to the male–female polarity used in Traditional Wicca, this heterofocal aspect could be seen by some, both inside and outside, as heterosexist or outright homophobic. Gardner's fears of acts which could perhaps induce sexual feelings occurring between members of the same sex is now quite widely condemned as homophobic, even by many Traditional Wiccans. The Farrars' statement that they do not feel qualified to write about homosexuals in the Craft has also been seen by many as homophobic (though those who prefer that people qualified by identity speak on such matters, may well have quite the opposite view), and their suggestion that two men would be unlikely to work well together as witches, even more so. Even their declaring that they had no problem with gay or lesbian practitioners, would raise objections for the wording "assume the role of their actual gender" [Farrar & Farrar 1984], conflating gender identity with sexual orientation.

Counter to this, the emphasis on fertility is not exclusive to any other expression of sexuality in a practitioner's life. The role of fertility as source of crops, livestock, game, and children is celebrated, but this is not given as the sole context in which one may "make music and love, all in my praise" [Charge], and gays and lesbians depend upon fertility to be alive as much as straight people. There is, perhaps, a colouring added by the much publicized decrees of some Christian denominations, such as the Roman Catholic Church, on issues of contraception, fertility

157

treatments and homosexuality. Their condemnation of contraception, in particular, allows for sexual intercourse solely in a manner that is, at least theoretically, open to being part of the mechanism of fertility. Since few people in the Western world would be entirely ignorant of their position on such issues, this would create knowledge of a particular conflation of sexuality, fertility and religion, that does indeed condemn homosexuality, and which could colour assumptions about how any religion holding fertility to be important, would also view homosexuality.

Of course, the Roman Catholic Church does not generally consider itself to be a fertility cult! Indeed, the very prohibitions upon contraception and fertility treatments mentioned above demonstrate that it is inclined against the attempts to encourage fertility to work in ways that are to one's or one's tribe's advantage. The manner in which it comes to value fertility is quite different from a hearty celebration of it, but rather a concession to its necessity, within an Augustine context that otherwise limits all sexual experience.

Another heterofocal aspect of Traditional Wicca is the advantage seen in the High Priest and High Priestess being lovers or life-partners. Since that is not often possible for a gay High Priest or lesbian High Priestess, and would seem to devalue the homosexual attractions a bisexual High Priest or High Priestess may experience, this too could be viewed as homophobic. Ultimately though, it is seen as advantageous but not as necessary, and only advantageous for quite specific reasons. It is not appropriate for all straight High Priests and High Priestesses either (including Gardner, whose wife was not Wiccan), and has not impeded a very large number of gay, lesbian, and bisexual people, along with straight people in monogamous relationships

158

with people outside the Craft, from fulfilling those roles. That some in the Craft did see homosexuality among priests as problematic, does necessitate an examination of whether this is inherent to Traditional Wiccan practice, or depended merely upon prevalent homophobia in the wider culture. Leo Martello's account of a public disagreement between himself and the editor of *The Wiccan* magazine (now *Pagan Dawn*) points sharply towards the latter. While both engage the question of gay men and lesbians being involved in a fertility cult (examined and dismissed above), much of the commentary in *The Wiccan* is nonsensical, such as his statement that their contact service for seekers should not be used by homosexuals because, "we are NOT a queer's contact service [original emphasis]" [Martello 1972b]—a statement that is clearly much more of a jeer, than of any theological position.

The advantage in working couples also being lovers does, however, stand as one reason why gay or lesbian couples may wish to work witchcraft together. While that would stand outside of much Traditional Wiccan practice, some of the advantages of working with one's lover and life-partner would still pertain to homosexual working couples. Further, while the compatibility of gay men and lesbians working in a fertility cult has been defended above, this does not mean that some gay men and lesbians may not personally feel they are placed outside of the mechanisms of fertility by their sexuality (for that matter, straight people may also feel their relationship to their own sexuality does not relate much to how they perceive the cycles of fertility as operating). For this reason alone, the development of a witchcraft which does not relate to fertility as Traditional Wicca does, is perhaps inevitable. Finally, there has long been religious and mystical expressions of homosex as having its own mysteries, which would be an obvious

159

attraction to some gay, lesbian, and bisexual witches, along with other non-heteronormative roles in other cultures such as that of the two-spirits in some tribes in the Americas, and hijras in India, who hold a position outside of those roles normal for either men or women in those cultures.

The women-only nature of much Dianic practice, makes it an obvious basis for the development of a lesbian stream of witchcraft. If anything this is overstated, given that Dianics, and other Feminist witches, often find it necessary to point out that they are not a lesbian-only tradition [Buckland 1986]. Radical Fairies [Adler 1997] and the Minoan Brotherhood [Minoan] both stand as examples of traditions for gay men.

Perhaps more influential on the development of Innovative Witchcraft as a whole though, are streams which attempt to more comprehensively deal with the sexuality of both straight and gay practitioners. Feri's ecstatic nature has always enabled it to do so, and as seen above, the influence of Reclaiming on much Innovative Witchcraft has brought Feri elements into the meme-pool from which Innovative Witchcraft operates.

Feri is not a fertility cult, however. Standing on its own quite separate from Wicca, the place for expression of sexuality within it is completely different, and homosexual expression is not at odds with any heterofocal elements. Where people take a large Wiccan influence, along with such moves to accommodate homosexual expression, matters can get more complex.

One such attempt used rites which alter the Traditional pairing of athamé and cup, to allow for a pairing of two athamés, or two cups. To do so though, retroactively reinterprets the original pairing, so that it is not a procreative pairing, but purely a sexual one. As well as removing much of the original symbolism, it could also lead to those traditions, including much Innovative practice, that allows only for the pairing of athamé and cup, to be misunderstood in the newly created context; a misunderstanding where it would be unfairly seen as homophobic, when it is really operating with a different meaning.

An easier way to deal with any such concerns though, is to simply downplay all sexual aspects until the potential issues no longer exist. Many Innovative publications simply omit all reference to sexuality, fertility-based or otherwise. D. J. Conway stands as quite remarkable in the degree to which she not only actively moves away from any sexual aspects, but assumes that such attitudes will find many like minds. As noted above she states "In my opinion, Gardner seems to have been obsessed with nudity, sex, and scourging, traits that may not have appeal to other Witches." Leaving aside the issue of scourging, as already examined, the two matters left are nudity and sex. Nudity is very much not highlighted in any form of Wicca or witchcraft that I have come across. To highlight nudity, one would need to place it in a context where others are dressed.[64] This is not the norm of any form of skyclad ritual, where if anything one person might be made a focus by being *temporarily* robed, rather than the other way around. At most, such an unbalance is rarely used in initiatory experiences. Considerations of Conway's statement about nudity can therefore, probably be folded into what her statement says

---

64 Hence when nudity is fetishized, it is generally in a context such as public exposure, forced nudity, nude male/clothed female, naked servants, etc., which all highlight it by putting it in an unbalanced situation. Even the most vanilla sexual representations of nudity reflect this, with stripteases involving people becoming naked, rather than being naked, and soft-pornographic nudes, of the kind found in British tabloids, capitalizing on the relative rarity of nakedness in their culture.

about sex. It is here that we find the strangest accusation. Compared with such fertility practices as copulating amongst growing corn, Wicca's use of sexual symbolism is very restrained. An accusation of obsession with something needs more justification than it merely being *referenced*. At most, we can detect not an obsession with sex, but merely an interest. I would suggest that such an interest is shared by the majority of people, indeed the majority of higher animals. Even if fertility aspects are abandoned, to suggest that many people would not still have an interest in sexual matters, seems to require a much greater defence. A further reflection of much the same attitude comes when she describes the well-known sexual symbolism of the besom as "notorious" [Conway 2001].

Where does this suggestion of *notoriety* come from? While Conway may perhaps be atypically prudish among Innovative Witches, it seems unlikely that such talk of notoriety can be merely a case of false consensus bias on her part and nothing else. Again, concern about sexual elements of Wicca being viewed negatively has been expressed in Wiccan writing since Gardner's: "I have been told by witches in England: 'Write and tell people we are not perverts'...." The difference is not in perceiving that there could be a problem, but in the solution found. Explaining the sexual elements of the Craft dispels some unfair accusations, as will describing policies of propriety that individual practitioners may have, such as Stewart Farrar's reportage did for Alex Sanders [Farrar 1971]. Apart from those who will quite simply refuse to believe what is said in any case, there is also the simple fact that even the element of sexuality that does exist in the Craft, will meet disapproval in some quarters. With sufficiently high emphasis on making the Craft acceptable, a desire to remove what sexual elements do exist, can arise.

Another motivation can exist in the fear that people may use such sexual elements as a tool in seduction or coercion. This is both a genuine concern from the inside, and a fear of how the Craft may be perceived from the outside.

From the outside, the image of the magician unscrupulously seeking to use the Arts to seduce women has been with us since before Dr Faustus first set eyes on Gretchen. In creating a story of a malicious magic-worker, whether for propaganda, or merely as entertainment, one needs believable motives for wrong-doing, and lust has always been up there with greed and ambition as such motives go. In such manner, the motives of the likes of Faust are no different than villains from an Agatha Christie whodunnit, but their means introduces an uncanny element to their crimes; while a mundane criminal may commit rape, or be motivated to murder by the consequences of their own adultery, the supernatural rapist, whether a magician like Faust or a praeternatural creature like Dracula, has the ability to control their victims at the level of their own psyche, reflecting fears of losing control in one's life to circumstance, or to unvoiced desires. The fear therefore strikes a deeper nerve.

Outside of the realm of fantasy, there have long existed cults whose leaders exercised an extreme degree of sexual control over practitioners. The 1990s saw considerable interest paid to such abuse occurring within the larger established Christian Churches, or criticism against the sexual control they maintained, in what they *prevented* practitioners from engaging in. History has seen allegations made against new or small groups, ranging from the absurd (the classic allegation of the orgy following the rite and feast

163

made by the Roman authorities against Christians, and later forming a central theme in the mediaeval story of the witches' Sabbath), to the far better documented (the fringe-Mormon underage marriage scandal *State of Utah v. Warren Steed Jeffs* [Utah 2008] which received a great deal of media attention).

This has a dual effect upon the Craft. The first, is that it colours assumptions people are wont to make in relation to *any* religious grouping, especially if small. The second, is that the Craft's self-perception of itself as valuing freedom, and hence as having very little internal control, leads its practitioners to view themselves not just as being completely removed from the cults which sporadically grab media attention, but as even further removed from them than are most other religions. The effect therefore is both on public perception of the Craft, and internal perception of what that public perception is. This cannot help but influence how witches, Traditional and Innovative alike, write and speak about their Craft, and hence they would inevitably pre-empt possible accusations of the Craft being used for sexual exploitation, which in turn would influence how successors were to write, and so on.

Meanwhile, Feminists in the Craft would also have had an influence. Such examples of sexism as Stokely Carmichael's statement that "Women's position within the SNCC is on their backs",[65] the survival of conservative gender roles into radical politics complained of by Marge Piercy in "In the Men's Rooms" [Piercy 1972], and the sort of gender issues within the New Left highlighted in Robin Morgan's "Goodbye to All That" [Morgan 1970], all taught Feminists that when it came to other movements they were involved with, they would not be able to assume

---

65 His exact words were "the position of women in SNCC is prone," but most commentators seem to assume he meant "supine" rather than "prone."

freedom from sexual harassment and exploitation, but must work to ensure this was so themselves. It would have been foolish to assume that any form of Paganism would not contain much the same problems, without an active pressure to ensure it didn't.

And finally, as numbers involved in Pagan witchcraft specifically, and Neopaganism generally, grew, the chances that there would indeed be sexual predators within the community naturally increased. The self-selecting nature, all the more pronounced the wider the definitions one is using, meant that there was nothing in the way of formal sanctions to prevent such behaviour taking place. The only real weapons available to those who would ensure that it did not, is to work to establish an intolerance for such behaviour as a cultural norm within the communities, and to warn members, especially newcomers, to be on their guard for the possibility.

In such a context, even the most oblique reference to sexuality could seem inappropriate to someone developing or adapting their own practice of witchcraft, and even more so should it come to be published in a description, or in a how-to guide on how others could make use of that same practice. Statements would be made with one eye on a hypothetical hostile critic and one eye on a hypothetical potential victim of abuse, while struggling also to discourage a hypothetical reader who would indeed be inclined to take just such an opportunity to abuse. A tendency to downplay the sexual aspects of the religious rites (and even more so the possibility of using sex-magic), would be natural, since any attempt to convey a genuine impression of the reality of the Craft must consider possible preconceptions on the part of the audience, and downplaying such aspects could indeed result in a more accurate portrayal overall.

165

It is hard to say just how real the danger of such abuses is. Human nature being as it is, the idea that almost nobody has ever expressly attempted to use pagan or occult interests as a front to allow sexual conquests or worse, would seem infeasible. The fact that sexual relationships do develop both within the Craft, and within the wider Pagan community, from brief flings to long-lasting marriages, also brings with it the risk for abuse that occurs within relationships that start consensually, and of heavy-handed attempts to form them, that happen in the wider community.

While there are some well-documented cases, the majority of claims of such instances are very much anecdotal. More than a few contain a fair degree of mocking comedy. One example from a web-based discussion group aimed at mocking aspects of Pagan culture [Peregrine 2007], aside from deriving humour from the incompetence of the attempt at seduction, contains several classic elements of the "foolish fluffy" story; goth sub-culture style of dress, use of the *Necronomicon* as a source, mispronunciation of *athamé*, and a naïf pretending to expertise. In this case the point is as much to condemn such folly, as any sexual misconduct, but such elements often appear in such stories; they are tales of the naïve preying on the even more naïve, rather than of cunning Svengali-like manipulators.

Does this mean that these stories are repeated or perhaps even created, purely for comic effect? It could be that such comic versions of the story are safer to repeat; we can laugh at the culprit and so reduce the fear of him. It could also reflect a moral philosophy where wrongdoing is seen as always foolish, and so the tale must demonstrate this. As such, the choice of evidence people choose to use in describing the potential for abuse, is itself coloured by a desire to downplay it.

166

Since works build on those works prior to them, this downplaying of the sexual aspects of the Craft will inevitably increase as time goes on, as later generations of writers are not just downplaying, but were introduced to witchcraft by resources which had already downplayed them. The stage is set for the uneasy descriptions of sexual symbolism in Conway, or for Ravenwolf's infamously sexist and puritan description of loss of virginity as *impure*: "the traditional colors for Mayday are red and white, representing the blood that flows from the woman when her purity is taken" [Ravenwolf 1993].

The development of a public face of witchcraft aimed at children and teenagers, increases the perceived value of a form of witchcraft without any overt expression of sexuality, neither in terms of its role in fertility, nor the ecstatic, nor any other.

In the meantime, while it may be pressure to be more acceptable to a wider community that has led to sexuality being de-emphasized in representations of witchcraft, that same increase in acceptance has given witches access to areas of the media that already have their own sexual mores. Fiona Horne's *Magickal Sex: A Witches' Guide to Beds, Knobs and Broomsticks* [Horne 2002] and *Bewitch a Man: How to Find Him and Keep Him Under Your Spell* [Horne 2006], Stella Damiana's *Sex Spells: the Magical Path to Erotic Bliss* [Damiana 2005], Stacey Demarco's *Witch in the Bedroom: Proven Sensual Magic* [Demarco 2006] and LaSara Firefox's *Sexy Witch* [Firefox 2006], each take slightly different approaches to the intersection of sex and witchcraft, but are all marketed rather similarly. Ironically, this may not so much be a backlash, as the filling of a vacuum; the desexualization of Wicca having left a *tabla rasa*, onto which commercialized sex can more easily be projected.

Chapter Ten

Churches, Incorporation, and Ministries

"I did not see why the schoolmaster should be taxed to
support the priest, and not the priest the schoolmaster."
—Henry David Thoreau,
"On the Duty of Civil Disobedience"

While Traditional Wicca has no laity, its priests and priestesses do
often serve ministerial roles to fellow priests, in such regards as
performing nuptial and funereal rites, as well as some performing
these roles for cowans. Innovative Witches have not only followed
suit, but are probably leading the trend in this regard. The effect
this has upon Traditional Wicca is minimized by the fact that no
such public rites are part of the Traditional liturgy, which may
not always hold true for Innovative practices.

The legal implications of doing so, varies considerably from
jurisdiction to jurisdiction. Some jurisdictions allow ministers of
any religion to register to be able to perform weddings that are
also recognized as state weddings, some allow for no such overlap
between religious and state authority and require all weddings to
be registered separately to any religious ceremony, some jurisdictions have a state religion which has precedence over others, and
some allow the ministers of the largest religions in their
jurisdiction to register legal marriages, as a matter of logistical
convenience.

The political implications of being allowed or denied the right to do so, necessarily depends on which of these cases is in effect. To not be allowed to where no other religious officiant can, clearly involves no discrimination, whereas being denied this in a jurisdiction where other religious officiants can, at the very least requires some further explanation from the authorities.

In serving people outside of one's coven, witches are acting in the same manner as ministers serving a laity. Just as the circumstances of solitary practitioners leads them to abandon the coven model, so too can there be a desire to go in the opposite direction, and move away from small tight groups of priests, which are at least nominally or potentially secret, towards completely adopting the model of a lay congregation being served by priests acting as ministers. If nothing else, the fact that having such a model of ministers serving a congregation is common in other religions, could suffice to make adoption of this model attractive to those familiar with them. The same can be said of dealing with such cases as hospital, prison, and military chaplaincies, where the mechanisms on the part of the civil authorities involved assume such models of ministry that are found in those religions predominant among those in their care.

Such models increase the advantages, or at least the perceived advantages, in obtaining whatever legal status other Churches have, in a given jurisdiction. Again, difficulty in doing so could be due to an instance of discrimination. However, even in the absence of any such difficulty, or in a jurisdiction where such difficulties could arise for other reasons, obtaining legal status (of just about any sort), for organizations, for individual officers of an organization, or for independently-operating ministers, is seen has having political value to the Pagan community.

While the examination of Identity Politics above focused on the question of *representations* of a given group, in the sense of how it is portrayed, two other focii of Identity-based analysis are *representation*, in the sense of the community in question being able to bring its concerns to various forums, and that of *recognition*.

> Recognition is at the heart of the matter.... Identity turns on the interrelated problems of self-recognition and recognition by others. Recognition is vital to any reflexivity, for example, any capacity to look at oneself, to choose one's actions and see their consequences, and to hope to make oneself something more or better than one is. This component of recognition may be the aspect of identity made most problematic by the social changes of modernity. (Calhoun 1994)

As such, a license to perform a wedding isn't solely of value because one can then perform a wedding, and obtaining a non-profit status for a religious organization isn't solely of value because one need then pay less tax. It is as important, if not even more important, in first requiring recognition from the authorities in question, and then standing as evidence of such recognition, that can be used in further battles for recognition.

Books aimed at beginners will often mention US Code 26 § 501(c)(3), the provision in the US Internal Revenue Code that exempts certain non-profit organizations from federal income taxes. The practical advantage of this is, of course, related to how much federal income tax an organization is paying, in turn related to how much income the organization has. For a small group where there is no tithing, and costs are met without the offices of a treasurer (for example, by people merely topping up any supplies they realize are low, or by round-robin, or pot-luck approaches), the advantage is nil. Yet beginners are being presented with such details of federal taxation of Churches, with Amber K's *Covencraft* [K 1998] even detailing questions her group had to deal with, in applying for 501(c)(3) status, from which one can only deduce, and expect the readers to deduce, that applying for such status is being encouraged, or at least suggested as likely to be of value.

Applying the same approach in other jurisdictions means doing so in a different context, where the value may differ. The Aquarian Tabernacle Church states that its Irish chapter, "received governmental recognition there as the first (and only) officially Wiccan/Pagan church in Ireland." [ATC] While there is such a recognized *organization* in Ireland, a State cannot recognize a *religion* when its constitution says, "The State guarantees not to endow any religion," [Article 44.2.2 of *Bunreacht na hÉireann*] and in particular had removed previous statements recognizing particular religions:

44.1.2 The State recognizes the special position of the Holy Catholic Apostolic and Roman Church as the guardian of the Faith professed by the great majority of the citizens.

44.1.3 The State also recognizes the Church of Ireland, the Presbyterian Church in Ireland, the Methodist Church in Ireland, the Religious Society of Friends in Ireland, as well as the Jewish Congregations and the other religious denominations existing in Ireland at the date of the coming into operation of this Constitution. (Bunreacht na hÉireann prior to the Fifth Amendment, 1972).

In light of this, the *removal* of recognition of certain religions by the Fifth Amendment to the Constitution of Ireland, stands as an important step in bringing the Irish state to a position that is likely more comfortable for Pagans than it was prior to 1972, and attempts to seek recognition from the state are perhaps a step backwards. American witches have sought to acquire artefacts of recognition that other religions enjoy, it does not follow that witches elsewhere should necessarily follow suit, given that the artefacts of such status will differ.

Chapter Eleven

Looking for the Warp and the Weft

"How can I know what I think until I see what I say?"
—E. M. Forster, *Aspects of the Novel*

I was reminded very quickly into beginning this work that the word *essay* originally meant an attempt and came from *essayer*, 'to try'. The act of writing it, and of trying to manage my tendency to parenthetical diversions in my thinking (the quotations at the start of each main chapter are there originally to give voice to some of my more irrelevant thoughts, so they would let me get back to my point), led to some surprises, and quite a different result than what I expected the attempt to bring.

Initially, I was motivated by my experience of having had some great, as well as some poor, experiences with Innovative Witchcraft, before committing to Traditional Wicca. I wanted to look back at why I both found value in some Innovative practices, and did not in others, from my current perspective, and see if I could find anything that could be extended to something more widely applicable, than to just my own experience. To do so though, is probably not possible through any analytical approach; what is most important in any form of witchcraft, is that which cannot be explained or expressed so directly, but which at most can only be conveyed by what Joyce Carol Oates calls "the prism of technique" [Oates 1992]. It needs artistry rather than exposition,

173

and at the cost of inevitably involving more bad poetry emerging from the Pagan community, attempts at this are certainly worth making, though this is not the place for it. At the very least, it needs a more emotional approach than that taken here.

Another difficulty with taking this approach to such a question, is that many Innovative Witchcraft practices are entirely intuitive in their bases; their core features do not come from, or end up in, any book or other textual resource.[66] In some cases, such an approach can be used as an excuse to avoid study, but it also covers some particularly impressive witches. Alas, by its very nature, such a very intuitive way of working does not leave much behind in the form of artefacts that can be examined by the sort of approach taken here, and as such as it is inevitably excluded, as unfair as that must be.

By the time I came to draft an outline, my original goal was already abandoned. The essay I then envisioned at that point, was in turn rapidly destroyed the moment I started actually writing.

One goal at that stage remained: namely to highlight features of both trends that may be missed when examining them together. It makes sense that, while speaking about witchcraft in the wider context of Western society, one would highlight those features that are outside of the norms of experience of post-Christian society—our worshipping a goddess as well as a god and our use of magic being two obvious examples—while examining them in relation to each other, should highlight different perspectives in either case, that will be of value to people

---

66 And this is also true for much that happens in even the most rigidly orthopraxic of Traditions, as well.

174

with an interest in either, or in both. Hopefully, I have achieved that, for some readers at least.

One continual problem throughout is that in each area of consideration, my method has resulted in my considering points of contrast, which despite continual attempts to indicate otherwise (at the cost of resulting in mealy-mouthed phrasing), there is a risk of implying that those points of contrast represent the entirety of Innovative Witchcraft. Since my perspective is that of a Traditional Wiccan, the result may be less balanced than I may wish for, particularly on those points where my previous practice was closer to the Traditional (and hence the other approach described is foreign to all that I have personally experienced). Where I did experience the point of difference in question as an Innovative Witch, and found it unsatisfying (and hence, while being able to claim a good position to judge its value in one way, in another I could be held to have a double bias against it), my perspective may likewise lack balance. Throughout this, I have striven to avoid bias, yet whether I genuinely succeeded in this or not—and it is impossible for me to judge my success here—the work as a whole reads to me as having a harsher view of Innovative Witchcraft than I actually hold to. Whether I should consider this to be a failure on my part, or an indication of finding something in the act of writing, or indeed if this harshness is really there at all—what reads to me as describing a difference where some forms of Innovative Witchcraft compare unfavourably to Traditional Wicca, may read to such Innovative witches as describing them more favourably in the comparison—is something on which I cannot offer much opinion.

Another problem with this work, is a tendency to focus upon the U.S., all the more problematic since I have no first-hand experience of that country. To a large degree, this is appropriate; much of the trends within Innovative Witchcraft originate in the U.S., and were re-imported into Europe in time to have a considerable influence on European witches of my generation. Another reason though, is that the easiest means to tell that a form of witchcraft that isn't Traditional Wicca, has at least a degree of post-Gardnerian influence, is the very use of the word *Wicca* that in part prompted this work. The influence of forms of witchcraft completely outside of Wicca in England, and the interest in local traditions in the Celtic Fringe countries, including my native Ireland, mean that the word is not as much used outside of its original sense here, and hence detecting post-Gardnerian influence outside of Traditional Wicca is not as straightforward. In all, while it is inevitable that forms of witch-craft influenced by Traditional Wicca, but outside of it, existed outside of the U.S. for the period examined, the practice of actually identifying these streams as *Wicca*, would seem to be an American one. There is still undoubtedly much that would inform this work that could be found outside of the Americas, particularly in England.

In this final section of conclusions, I shall indulge in *not* attempting objectivity, as I have done earlier, but allow my own opinions greater voice.

11.1 Identity Politics and Teens

My first surprise, is that I found myself writing more on politics that I imagined I would, something I have mixed feelings about as a former (and rather ineffectual) activist, who has quite consciously abandoned explicit activism. Yet the position of Identity Politics in how modern witchcraft is discussed, and how modern witches, particularly young people developing an interest in the Craft, view their position cannot be ignored. The important question, is whether and in what way this politics feeds back into their witchcraft. Certainly, the view exists that a motivation for "fluffies" is, "to make a political statement" [Nobel Beyer 2002], but that polarized position is not a promising source for a balanced view of just how this may operate in practice. Indeed, the very concept of fluffiness can be a way of policing an identity. Since the rejection of any concept of initiatory lineage allows for no formal means of determining who is, or is not, considered Wiccan within Innovative Witchcraft, those who are seen as claiming to be "us", but as not, or as "us", but of letting "us" down will be rejected by other means. Compare this with labels like, *Uncle Tom* within the African-American community, *ChuDWah* within fetish communities, and so on, along with some such as *Lipstick Lesbian*, that later became identities people would actively associate themselves with.[67] The anti-fluffy concept therefore, itself fits into an Identity Politics. That it does so in a negative manner, in defining what it is *against* more clearly than what it is *for*, has probably removed much of the impact of each individual argument made.

In looking at the portrayals that are of such great concern to the Identity Political analysis, along with generating interest even in the mainstream press, I have to conclude that there is no doubt something of real impact here, but that more red herrings than

---

67 For that matter, a great many labels that are now the most commonly used names for religious and political groups started as insults, including *Tory*, *Whig*, *Quaker*, and indeed, *Gardnerian*.

insights are on offer. That one popular culture representation can be read as commenting on this very Identity Politics, makes that series seem particularly rich in subtext, and worth another view generally, but the question it raises about whether such attachment to a politicized identity can lead to a loss of authenticity, rather than a gain, remains unanswered. The safest prediction for where the teen witches of today will be, some ten years or so from now, is that some will still be engaging in some sort of Craft, and being very accomplished at what they are doing, while others will indeed find that witchcraft gave them an identity they could hide themselves in, rather than find anything of true value in. Alas, stating this is little more than spouting a truism, unless an unprejudiced means to predict who will be likely to find that they are truly called to witchcraft could be be developed.

The question of how, if at all, adult witches can help these teen witches is also something I cannot come to any firm conclusions on. I certainly find little of much value in the resources marketed at them. Informationally, there is nothing here that is not already easily available elsewhere, and I feel pretty confident in saying that the tone would have greatly irritated me at that age. Finally, they lack guts when it comes to anything that addresses the situations that teenagers find themselves having to cope with.

The resources teenagers provide for themselves, are much more promising in many ways. They may often read as naïve, but I am inclined suggest that it is better to give young people opportunities for creativity. There may not be many Shelleys, Brontës, Rimbauds, or Mozarts in the world, but there are enough that dismissing what teenagers may have to bring out of hand, may be unwise.

At the same time there seems to be a strong incentive to avoid stating one particular observation: *Teenagers' judgement sucks.* Whether it's from some sort of political correctness,[68] or an understanding that young people are likely to resent such an opinion, and hence not listen to anything else one has to say after they hear one express it, or maybe just that people don't want to make their own judgements fair game for comment,[69] this is rarely expressed outright. Yet in traditions that value wisdom and often honour the Crone aspects of the divine, is it really inappropriate, just to point out that teenagers do not, as a rule, make very good judgements? To attempt to grow in a manner appropriate for a witch, would young people not perhaps be best advised to examine the ways in which they, and their peers, tend to make judgements? Can something be done that assists them in this, while at the same time not descending to the patronizing tone of existing resources?

When young people have ambitions to any other endeavour, whether vocational or avocational, that requires an ongoing commitment, and is also generally an adult pursuit, then whether they can engage in it at that time, or have to wait until an older age, there is most often quite a bit of ground work that can, or must, be done beforehand. Considering that any youths interested in the Craft are presumably intending that they would continue with it long into their adult life, perhaps this ground-work should focus on what will aid them best in later pursuit of the Craft, than presently.

---

68 An ever-problematic term, but here I need not deal with the question of the value of *political correctness*, or even if it really exists, just that the concept exists in some form, and influences public behaviour of many.

69 And teenagers are often annoyingly good at finding flaws in adults' judgement, at the best of times.

Thinking back to my own teenage years (I did not have an interest in Wicca then, though given my range of interests at the time, it sometimes seems strange that I never did research it more), what I feel I could have done then, that would be of most benefit to my practice now, would include paying better attention to learning languages in school. This is not something to be found in any book on witchcraft, but it was something offered to me at the tax-payers expense, and with stronger adult encouragement than I would have liked at the time! Developing better ability at memorizing verse—already going out of fashion in my day but still present in the English Literature curriculum—would also have helped. Better habits regarding physical fitness would also have been of benefit. Indeed, I probably retain a bias against acknowledging just how much, considering how long it is since I've been to the gym.

The first thing I think of that moves out of what was already offered by my grammar-school education, is basic meditative technique: something I did work on at the time, but not with much resolution. Another would be some sort of martial art, especially one with a concept of *chi* or similar. Even with this, the curriculum suggested here is still some way away from anything that is making it into the teen-marketed resources on witchcraft. Similarly, if I come to think about what did stand me in stead from that part of my life, it is not the limited occult and mystical research I engaged in at the time. Perhaps a curriculum of suggested training could be developed, that would benefit future witches in later practice, while also working well with their formal education. Such a curriculum would also be general enough to have benefits for those who no longer feel called to practice witchcraft when they get older, be relatively uncontroversial with

180

parents, and the lack of surface sparkle may well be reassuring to some.

11.2 Apolitical Traditions Revisited

Moving back to politics, I was particularly surprised at how much attention I found myself paying to WITCH, as I must admit I previously thought of them as little more than a footnote in the history of both witchcraft and Feminism, due to how short-lived they were. In addition to my learning that Robin Morgan's influential "Goodbye To All That" was written during the period, I find many points of similarity with later Feminist witchcraft. Many seem superficial, but they may have been very powerful in planting memes that later grew into a Feminist use of witchcraft that took that witchcraft more seriously.

One criticism that is made of politicized witchcraft is their previous, and in some cases, persisting, belief in a matriarchal prehistory, and in the account of the Burning Times popularized by Matilda Joslyn Gage. Such criticism attacks both the religious and political theory at the same time.

Both Feminists and witches have been able to absorb the changes to how academically acceptable these theories have become. Continuing belief (or at least continuing *uncritical* belief) in them is now rare, and articles critical of them are as often found in publications explicitly favouring Feminist or Wiccan views.[70] Combinations of the two seem to have a harder time absorbing such changes in scholarly opinion. Starhawk's notes to

---

70 To have cowans singing about the historical oppression of witches, while witches write articles on witchvox.com about this being both exaggerated, and unrelated to modern witches, must stand one of the more amusing ironies in Identity Politics.

her latest addition of *The Spiral Dance* recognize that the death toll of the Burning Times was "probably" much lower than the nine million cited, but falls a great deal short from accepting the latest research in this regard.

An analogy could perhaps be made, with the preference of engineers for "loosely coupling" very separate devices, and that of marketers for integrating them tightly. If you combine several useful or desirable items together, it is easier to convince other people of their value, but if you keep everything separate, and interacting only at particular points of contact, then it is easier to fix, improve, replace, or discard, any one of them, without damage to the rest of the system.

A great many Traditional Wiccans have been involved in a great many political causes, including Feminist and environmental causes, and do not seem to have the same difficulties in adapting to change of historical opinion, in either their religious or political life. Perhaps the traditional apolitical stance of the old magical orders is actually an advantage, rather than an impediment, to those who feel called to political action. An ideology that ties witchcraft to political thought could be seen as providing a single point of failure for both.

John Rowan criticized Wicca and witchcraft by arguing "the Craft was not designed to overthrow patriarchy, it was designed to ignore patriarchy" [Rowan 1987]. Politically-active witches, whether Traditional, Innovative, or non-Wiccan, may feel otherwise, but perhaps his criticism points to a strength, rather than a weakness, for those who feel called to both Pagan witchcraft and political action against patriarchy. While a religious perspective that ignores patriarchy will not entail support for such action, and mean that one cannot necessarily count upon one's co-religionists

182

and coven siblings as comrades, neither is it in direct opposition to such politics, as many would argue many other religions are.

As such, if we accept Rowan's criticism of the Craft, there is still arguably less conflict in reconciling Feminist or ecological politics, and other political positions besides, and Traditional Wicca, or forms of witchcraft that share its apolitical position, than in reconciling them with those religions that Feminists have criticized as perpetuating patriarchy, and which radical ecologists have criticized for supporting a view of natural resources that justifies unrestrained exploitation.

Some politically-motivated Innovative Witches may therefore find greater value in emulating Traditional Wicca's lack of explicit politics, than in emulating the joined-up philosophy of Starhawk or Budapest. Such an approach will never satisfy everyone for whom political, religious, and magical expression are each important, but it may become a more common combination, as understandings of ideas that have been important to political witches change (whether the changes come from academia or elsewhere), and these changes must be either resisted or absorbed, in both the political and religious sphere.

The criticism of much politicized witchcraft as "fluffy" will probably be both an encouragement and impediment to such a move: an encouragement in altering the cultural landscape of Paganism, so as to be more critical of some of the views behind politicized witchcraft, but an impediment in this leading to a staunchly anti-Feminist stream in Pagan thinking, and perhaps also a backlash to environmentalists' recent successes, which could create a fault line that divides Pagan culture quite sharply, and lead to a degree of polarized insularity on both sides.

11.3 The Value of Lip Service

More than once, I came to the conclusion that the reason for a piece of terminology or a practice being used in Innovative Witchcraft, is that it is seen as a "Wiccan word" or a "Wiccan thing". To some Innovative Witches this may seem disparaging, especially if, as I have argued above that many do, they place doctrine in a position where it precedes praxis. However, I see considerable value in such artefacts; this is what tradition is, in a sense. There is also a certain regard for the poetry of such phrases, and the beauty of practices, that I feel is important. Of course, Innovative Witchcraft is also developing its own nomenclature that contains other terms and expressions, such as *solitaire*, for a solitary practitioner, and *Book of Mirrors*, for a book solely for recording dreams and experiences, rather than techniques or other knowledge acquired elsewhere. Opinions will of course differ in each case (personally I find *solitaire* hopelessly inaccurate in historically implying reclusion, but I find *Book of Mirrors* to be lovely in its evocative phrasing). Some of these terms will die out while others thrive.

For Innovative Witches who wish to benefit from what is public about Traditional Wicca, perhaps what is needed is not *less* lip-service, like some argue in the face of activities they see as superficial, but *more*. Thinking of the abandonment of the scourge in much Innovative Witchcraft, I wonder if perhaps merely placing it on the altar unused, would be better than removing it entirely. If a given practitioner sees no value in it, is it necessarily wise to prevent it from becoming part of a downline's practice?

This would still radically downplay the scourge's position, but to de-emphasize a tool has a precedent in Traditional Wicca:

At first I was puzzled by the absence of the Cup from the witches' working tools and the inclusion of the unimportant pentacle,....

The answer I get is: In the burning times this was done deliberately. Any mention of the Cup led to an orgy of torture, their persecutors saying that it was a parody of the Mass; also the riding or dancing pole ('broomstick') was cut out. Censer and pentacle were substituted and explanations made to fit what their persecutors expected. If all told more or less the same story of what they were taught—because it was actually true and it agreed with the story of others—why bother to continue the torture? (Gardner 1954).

How different is this to removing the cup entirely! Furthermore, such witches knew that they were de-emphasizing the cup, which does not apply to someone studying their Craft from books that have either silently omitted the scourge, or explained it away as nothing more than an artefact of one man's sexual peccadilloes. The most essential difference, remains that the manner in which Gardner tells us the cup was removed from one place it could have been mentioned, potentially reduced information only to cowans, or to newcomers who would be expected to learn more about it soon, whereas the manner in which so many Innovative writers have removed the scourge from the Craft, retained information from would-be practitioners. At this point, the absence of the scourge in much Innovative Witchcraft is now a persistent legacy of those who rejected it, and it is simply not much considered, or often even known of, by those who follow in their wake.

On the other hand, what value the scourge has for any Innovative practice will depend on that practice, and it is not my place to comment. Having done so, I may as well go on to opine

185

that a greater attention to non-Wiccan streams of witchcraft could also perhaps benefit many. I can see Ann Finnin's *The Forge of Tubal Cain* [Finnin 2008], for example inspiring many that are defining their own practice.

11.4 Sexuality

The explanation of the scourge's use existing purely out of a sado-masochistic desire, is one I find hard to buy. As BDSM becomes more openly expressed in our society, I believe the argument will become harder to justify still, unless the scourge proves more popular within it than I suspect it will. Scourges simply aren't terribly popular in constructing "scenes". Even if a sexual interest did form a motivation as the allegation says, it doesn't suffice to explain the use of a scourge, rather than a switch or birch-rod, or much of the way in which scourge is used. To persuade people that any given English gentleman of Gardner's generation, was engaging in "the English vice" has been an easy task, due to how it fitted with late twentieth century stereotypes of Victorian-era sexuality, and of BDSM itself, despite his non-institutional educational background probably insulating him from much of the alleged causes—the stereotype being of such preferences being formed due to the English education system, which Gardner didn't attend. There is currently a fashion for re-appraising attitudes towards the Victorian era generally, and I feel that this, combined with changes in the image of BDSM, will soon make the allegations seem not just unsupportable, but quaintly naïve.

The prudishness of Conway in particular, I honestly find quite shocking. It is rather extreme though, and perhaps it is unfair to Innovative witchcraft generally to pay her example too much attention. To ignore her example, though, is likely unfair also.

Differing views of the question of the place of sexuality in witchcraft points to larger questions of just what is witchcraft meant to be, and how it should present itself.

11.5 Expectations

The first question ("What is witchcraft meant to be?") is perhaps the ultimate engine behind much change that happens within Innovative Witchcraft; I lack much insight into answers to that question on the part of Innovative Witches. If anything, I feel I have less of an idea here, than when I began. Things would get even more confusing if I were now to include traditions and trends that I deliberately excluded. In the first chapter I gave some reasons for excluding some such trends, such as those who consider themselves "Wiccan" but not witches. Returning to the boundaries I drew at the time, I have to question my own motives. While I had to have some criteria for inclusion or exclusion, and stand by the restriction to forms of witchcraft, I also realise that part of my motivation was simply that I have too great a difficulty in seeing such people as even vaguely related to anything I would label *Wicca*.

Such decisions being made by other people, can perhaps be detected by what they find humorous. The first I ever heard about the Correlian Nativist Church, was from Wiccans who found them funny, yet such things as the robes, school, and organizational structure that will strike some as strange, wouldn't do so if they were a Druid order or a Christian denomination; it is the contrast with what people expect from Wicca, that causes them to find humour in the incongruity. Much the same may be true of Innovative Witches who value their view of Wicca as being free-form and spontaneous, and cannot reconcile that view with descriptions of Traditional Wicca, so similarly finding humour there.

This humour is found in incongruity when the clash between expectation and result happens immediately, and sharply. When the disparity takes longer to surface the reactions can be more unpleasant. It is said that "expectations are premeditated resentments".[71] Of course expectations proving incorrect may merely elicit humour, as above, or indeed delight, depending on the circumstance. It is when expectations are allowed to grow or otherwise be invested in, that their being dashed can result in resentment. Differences between different forms of witchcraft, whether across Traditional/Innovative lines, or otherwise, can bring a mixture of considered criticism and debate, insight and inspiration, or can merely be interesting to learn about. But someone shaken by an unmet expectation is wont to experience resentment that could encourage not discussion, but mere sectarianism.

Expectations can collapse on both sides simultaneously, and in different ways. I witnessed an online discussion on aspects of Wicca which started with one person making Traditional assumptions, and arguing in terms of Wicca being a fertility cult. One respondent indignantly retorted "Since when has Wicca been a fertility cult?" To some this response seemed as absurd as "Since when has water been wet?" To others he seemed to have hit upon the *mot juste* to counter nonsense, written by someone who clearly knew nothing about Wicca! Perhaps, depending on how they viewed the expression *fertility cult* (particularly in light of recent colourings of the word *cult*), some even saw the opening statements

---

71   This saying seems to be popular in Alcoholics Anonymous. The source may
be Peck 2002.

as anti-Wicca. Expectations were clearly departed from on both sides, and resentment did indeed emerge in the participants' tone.

With Traditional Wicca being in the exalted position of being the elder of Innovated Witchcraft, and in many ways its progenitor, but Innovative Witchcraft being in the likewise exalted position as the larger, more visible, and more diverse of the two, neither is ever going to be able to completely ignore the other. With interaction being inevitable, such interaction can only be conducive to anything other than discord if expectations of the other are realistic. Neither can expect the other to fit their definition of *Wicca*, and must be prepared for surprises when confronted with departures from their own practice. But neither can expect the other to fit comfortable stereotypes that reflect details of those differences.

The second question ("How witchcraft should present itself?") seems often a point of more vocal disagreement than the core differences underneath. Apart from influencing the concern about reportage and fictional representations, this question also heavily influences the view within witchcraft of anyone who allows themselves to be so reported, or makes any public statements. Any such act potentially alters the interface between the Craft and the public—but so does deliberately avoiding such publicity.

This question then becomes reified into the question of whether paying any attention to how outsiders may view something could place one's focus other than where it should be; that focusing on the values of outsiders removes focus from one's own values. With the only absolute position possible being that of strict secrecy, and all other positions by necessity being differences in degree, it is inevitably going to remain fraught. Underscoring all of this is the growing position of the Pagan community as a market, with the potential both for increasing commercialization and increasing suspicion of commercial motives.

11.6 Nature

After the eight Sabbats, Earth Day is probably the most mentioned date on Witchvox.com and other forums of Wiccan discussion. That Wicca is a nature religion, seems to be treated as self-evident by many Innovative Witches.

In examining the question of whether this is true of Traditional Wicca, I eventually concluded that the very question is pretty much irrelevant. One can certainly define *nature religion* in such a way as to include all, or almost all, Traditional Wiccans, so somebody may find it useful in a descriptive manner. Where people seek to start from *nature religion* in determining what Wicca is, or what it "should" be, then this not only repeats the act of assuming doctrine precedes praxis, that I hold to be of little value with Traditional Wicca, but also allows one to define *nature religion* as one wants. In the end, I could not only find no final answer to the question, but no value in answering it.

11.7 The W-Word

The question raised at the start of this work, is that around the use of the word *Wicca* by Innovative witches. At the end of it, I find myself less inclined to be tolerant of such usage than I was before. I started this work as a Traditional Wiccan, who uses *Wicca* and *The Wicca* as they are used within its Traditions. Before that, I had been an Innovative Witch, who used the word *witch*, and preferred it over *Wiccan* in quite a few ways.[72] Yet despite this I

---

72 I can't claim too much in the way of foresight in this regard, part of my
    reason for avoiding *Wicca*, was that I had the mistaken belief that those

was inclined, due to a general predisposition towards taking a descriptive rather than prescriptive view of the English language, to consider this a valid usage, albeit not one that I would ever share.

A descriptive view of language can only go so far, though. If taken to extremes it descends into meaninglessness. If the word *wicca* is to be of any use, it must mean something, and the degree of variety within post-Gardnerian practice generally means that outside of its original usage it tends to end up meaning anything, and hence meaning nothing. Added to this, is a perception on my part that those forms of witchcraft, post-Gardnerian or otherwise, which do *not* use the word *Wicca* tend, ironically, to have more in common with Wicca as I understand it, than those that *do*.

In considering the question of when cultural borrowing crosses into cultural theft, I suggested that much of Innovative Witchcraft could be considered from a Traditional Wiccan perspective in much the same way. When considering this myself, I find it hard to logically argue any other way about the use of the label *Wicca* for something outside of the lineages from which it came, but nor can I say emotionally that I find this offensive, in the way that I as an Irishman do find *Witta* [McCoy 1993] and *Faery Wicca* [Stepanich 1994 & Stepanich 1998] to be offensive. Partly I suspect this is because it does not come on top of a prior colonial experience—but mostly, for all of our increasing visibility, the Wicca are still Her hidden children, and as such complaining loudly about a practice by outsiders that is not active persecution, is perhaps not an appropriate stance.

---

using the word, considered it an unbroken continuation from the Anglo-Saxon *wicca*.

Where I do find it problematic is in terms of the effect it has upon seekers, whether those seekers are seeking Traditional Wicca, Innovative Witchcraft, another form of witchcraft, or are unsure which one they are called to, if indeed they are called to any of them at all. Strangely enough, I find it more disparaging to Innovative Witchcraft (remembering that when I exclusively practised it myself, I did not use the term *Wicca*); to borrow the clothes of another practice carries an implication that it cannot stand on its own merits. This on its own would seem a strong reason not to extend the term in the manner in which it has been extended.

Since a word that means anything ends up meaning nothing, and our culture does not tolerate meaningless words,[73] I do not think continually straining *Wicca* to cover an increasingly wide range of practices can continue until it becomes a metasyntactic term for people to apply definition to as they wish, but eventually it must implode into a new, firmer, definition. Still, it seems that the word is too engrained in general usage outside of Britain and Ireland, and increasingly even there, for it to revert to its original meaning. Rather, I suspect that the term will be influenced by the existence of implicit orthodoxies I have pointed to in Innovative Witchcraft, and so it will come to be narrowed down to fit those orthodoxies, as they become strengthened by repetition and continuation. Ironically, this will likely result in the most popular definition of *Wicca* actually excluding those Traditional Wiccan practitioners who do not fit these orthodoxies. While the idea of

---

73 Consider that words coined without meaning for nonsense verse, such as *chortle* from Lewis Carroll's "Jabberwocky", and *runcible* from Edward Lear's "The Owl and the Pussycat" and "The Pobble Who Has No Toes" have since acquired quite precise definitions.

a definition of *Wicca* that actually excludes Gardnerians, Alexandrians, Mohsians, and so on may seem absurd, perhaps the greater severance between Traditional and Innovative practices this would entail, would lead to there being less disagreement between them; we tend to have greater grudges with closer neighbours. The overlap in the definitions is a key to the source of potential confusion. As such, in being a contentious signifier it seeds contention between the identities it signifies, with each feeling they are being silenced by the other. With two definitions that are not only separate, but seen as separate by both, and understood as separate by outsiders, then neither definition would entail this silencing.

Wicca itself is not the only term that is understood differently by both groups. In looking at differences around the *Book of Shadows*, it was clear that the concepts differ considerably even though the same term is used. *Tradition*, also, has overlapping but different meanings between the two trends, only some of which agree with the common dictionary senses.

Even words which don't have specific meaning to either trend are often used differently. Innovative criticisms of Traditional practices often refer to them as *dogmatic*, but strictly, dogmas are only tenets and beliefs, not practices, so it is not technically possible for anyone to be dogmatic in any practice, only in their beliefs about it. With a lack of dogma *valued* throughout much of modern Paganism generally, this ceases to be a mere lexical pedantry, and acquires significance and the potential for emotional impact. So too, differences in understanding of the terms *rede*, *initiation*, *training*, and *nature religion*, in their general senses will impact upon differences in attitudes to what they signify specifically within Pagan witchcraft. While the differences

193

aren't solely across the line between Traditional and Innovative, they frequently are. Given the way in which language shapes assumptions and expectations, these differences, especially if unacknowledged, are wont to lead to misunderstandings. As much as anything else, Traditional Wicca and Innovative Witch-craft are perhaps divided by a common language.

Appendix A

Glossary

Alexandrian: A denomination of Traditional Wicca, tracing back to Alex Sanders

American Council of Witches: A short-lived, though never officially disbanded, grouping of witches of disparate traditions and practices, primarily notable for releasing a declaration of "13 Principles of Wiccan Belief".

apotropaic: Having qualities which ward against evil or harmful influences.

Aquarian Tabernacle Church: A Pagan Church incorporated in Index, Washington.

Aradia: The goddess honoured by the witches described in Leland 1899, perhaps derived from Herodias, the mother of Salome, or from the folkloric 14th Century figure Aradia de Toscana, who some have suggested may have been historical. The name has been used as a public goddess name by some Traditional Wiccans.

Arcadia: A region in Greece (coincidentally, the birthplace of Pan). From late 19th Century, the term is used figuratively to refer to a pastoral ideal of rural life.

Ardanes: Laws of some traditions of Traditional Wicca.

athamé [ˈæθəmeɪ], [əˈθeɪmiː] ([əˈθeɪm] is frowned upon as incorrect): Also known as the black-handled knife, though some would not consider the colour of the handle important. Its uses are generally purely ritualized, and it is generally not used to cut.

besom [ˈbiːzəm]: A broom made of twigs bound to a stick.

boline [boʊˈliːn]: A sharp knife, traditionally white-handled. In contrast to the athamé it is used to cut, carve or inscribe.

British Traditional Wicca: A term proposed for what this work terms *Traditional Wicca*, mainly used in the US and Canada, but increasingly outside of those countries.

Burning Times, The: The period during which witchcraft was punishable by death, particularly the height of the witch-crazes. The term first appears in print in Gardner 1954, and in capitalized form in Daly 1978.

Cernunnos [ˌkɛɹˈnuːnəs]: A Celtic deity referred to in inscriptions found in modern France and Germany, with other representations throughout Europe claimed to be of the same god. The name has been used as a public god name by some Traditional Wiccans.

Charge of the Goddess: A declamation spoken as by a goddess in the first person, and spoken by the High Priestess after the Drawing Down of the Moon. The poetic and prose versions most strongly associated with Traditional Wicca are attributed to Doreen Valiente (see Farrar & Farrar 1984). Variations and alternative versions are found widely.

Clan of Tubal Cain: The coven Robert Cochrane worked in, in the 1950s. Several current groups claim lineage to this group or its ideas. All such groups generally do not consider themselves to be Wiccan.

Correlian Nativist Church: A Pagan Church incorporated in Albany, New York.

cowan: [ˈkoʊən] Originally stone-mason jargon and coming from them to witches via Freemasonry, *cowan* is used to refer to outsiders (*cf.* "gentile"). It is not clear whether the term as used by one group of witches would include some or all other witches. Here it is used only for those who do not identify as a witch of any type.

cunningman: A man who claims to be able to do folk-magic, for healing or other tasks. The term is first found in the seventeenth century, becoming rare in the last century though not dying out entirely.

Dianic: A label used by several denominations of Feminist witchcraft, particularly that founded by Zsuzsana Budapest, though the McFarland Dianic Tradition, and perhaps others, do not stem from her line.

Drawing Down the Moon: The act of invoking the goddess into a High Priestess. In Traditional Wicca, this is most often done by the High Priest acting so as to bring this invocation about. Outside of Traditional Wicca considerable variation exists both as to precisely what Drawing Down is said to involve and as to the mechanism used.

Eclectic: The term *Eclectic* is often used by Traditional Wiccans to describe other forms of witchcraft, especially those which to some extent were influenced by or otherwise derive from Traditional Wicca or particular Traditional Wiccans (that is, what in this work is termed *Innovative Witchcraft*). Among some other witches it is used to identify those forms of witchcraft which consciously and deliberately involve a high degree of syncretism.

essentialism: Ascribing characteristics as innate qualities rather than associated by culture, environment or other factors external to the thing or person in question. Essentialisms of several very different types are addressed in the course of this work, so the precise meaning differs from chapter to chapter.

Feri: A tradition of Pagan witchcraft with an ecstatic focus, stemming from the teachings of Victor and Cora Anderson.

Five-Fold Kiss: An element of Traditional Wiccan ritual in which a woman's feet, knees, womb, breasts and lips or a man's feet, knees, phallus, breast and lips are blessed with a kiss on or (in the case of the womb or phallus) near them.

Gardnerian: A Traditional Wiccan denomination tracing back to Gerard Gardner. Note that the Gardnerian Tradition is *post-Gardnerian* as that latter term is used in this work.

heterofocal: Focusing upon male–female pairings. Heterofocality is often an aspect of heterosexism (viewing things through heterosexual assumptions) and homophobia (actively opposed to or discriminatory against homosexuality), but it does not entail either of them and can arguably be present without heterosexism and homophobia.

High Priest: Either a priest of particular rank (generally 2° or 3°) or, specifically, the high priest who is taking the leading male róle in a ritual or in the running of a coven.

High Priestess: Either a priestess of particular rank (generally 2° or 3°) or, specifically, the high priestess who is taking the leading female role in a ritual or the running of a coven.

hijras: A "third gender" in South Asian culture.

Imbolc, Imbolg ['imbɔlk], ['imbɔlˠg]: An Irish festival mentioned in Kinsella 1970. The name is now often used by witches and other Pagans for the sabbat at the beginning of February, which Gardner referred to as Candlemas.

Iron Pentacle: One of several conceptual and meditative tools used in the Feri tradition.

Litha ['liːθə]: A term appearing in the Anglo-Saxon calendar for two months during the summer [Wallis 1999]. It has been adopted, possibly influenced by Tolkien's fictional Shire Calendar, as a term for the Summer Solstice. Relatively, the term is more popular among Innovative Witches than Traditional Wiccans.

Lughnasadh ['luːnəsə]: An Irish festival (see MacNeill 1982). The name, surviving in the Irish month name *Lúnasa*, is now often used by witches and other Pagans for the sabbat at the beginning of August, which Gardner referred to as Lammas.

Mabon ['mæbɔn] (['meibɔn] in North America): Mabon ap Modron ("Divine Son, son of Divine Mother") is a hero in the Welsh tale "Culhwch ac Olwen". The term Mabon has recently been adopted as a name for the Autumnal Equinox. Relatively, this term is more popular among Innovative Witches than Traditional Wiccans.

Mesopaganism: "Middle Paganism". A term used by Isaac Bonewits to describe modern forms of Paganism which emerged prior to the 1960s and which he claims are also influenced "accidentally, deliberately and/or involuntarily" by Western monotheist and nontheist concepts.

Mohsian: A denomination of Traditional Wicca tracing to Bill and Helen Mohs. Previously self-identified as *American Eclectic Wicca*, this name was dropped as *eclectic* came to be specifically associated with forms of witchcraft other than Traditional Wicca.

Murray Hypothesis: The theory put forth by Margaret Murray that mediaeval witchcraft was a survival of pre-Christian religous practice. This is often extended to suggesting that modern witchcraft is a survival in turn of mediaeval witchcraft, and hence by extension, of pre-Christian practice.

Neopaganism: "New Paganism". Either:

- Any modern form of paganism existing in cultures where such religions have not remained the predominant practice since pre-Christian times.

- Modern forms paganism from the 1960s and later that consciously strive to exclude elements of Western thought influenced by Western monotheism. [Bonewits 1979].

New Age Movement: A diffuse movement combining a variety of philosophies and practices in a highly syncretistic manner, and largely focussing on personal growth and spiritual accomplishment, often claiming related benefits for followers' health and prosperity.

New Forest: An area in South England (mostly south-west Hampshire, but also some of north-west Wiltshire). It was here that Gardner claimed to have first made contact with witches.

Orthopraxy: "Correct action". Behaving in accordance with a religion's rules; as opposed to orthodoxy, "correct belief/opinion", believing in a religion's teachings. Orthopraxy applies to both rituals specific to the religion, and to "every day" behaviour, and a religion may place different emphasis upon each.

Ostara [o'staɪə]: A name for the Vernal (Spring) Equinox derived from the goddess *Eostre*, mentioned by Bede [Wallis 1999]. Relatively, it is more popular among Innovative Witches than Traditional Wiccans.

Palaeopaganism: "Old Paganism," paganism as practised in pre-Christian times, rather than survivals, revitalizations or reconstructions.

pentacle: *Pentacle* may refer to a pentagram (five-pointed star, drawn as with a single line) especially if surrounded by a circle. It may also, especially in the variant pantacle [Jones 1974], refer to an amulet or magical tool of paper, metal or other material with symbols drawn upon it. The two senses overlap in the case of such an amulet or magical tool should the symbols primarily, or solely, feature a pentagram, as is commonly the case in post-Gardnerian witchcraft.

Post-Gardnerian: In my usage in this work, referring to the legacy and influence of Gerard Gardner. Hence including all Traditional Wiccans (including Gardnerians) along with all other witches that have inherited features from, or believed to be from, Traditional Wiccans, whether directly or indirectly.

Reclaiming: A denomination of witchcraft predominantly influenced by Feri, and much concerned with political action, particularly engaged with Feminist and environmental concerns.

reconstructionism: Forms of Neopaganism which put considerable emphasis upon reconstructing Palaeopagan practices as faithfully as possible, and hence considering scholarly research into those practices to be particularly important.

Rede: In general, a piece of advice. More specifically, the *Wiccan Rede*, of "An it harm none, do what thou wilt" and several variants.

Regency, The: One of many groups based on or inspired by the form of witchcraft practised by Robert Cochrane.

Sabbat: A seasonal celebration held on four or, more commonly, eight times throughout the year.

Glossary

Samhain: An Irish festival mentioned in Kinsella 1970. The name is now often used by witches and other Pagans for the sabbat at the end of October, which Gardner referred to as Halloween.

Seax-Wica ['sæks 'wɪkə]: A Tradition of witchcraft founded by Raymond Buckland in the 1970s that references Saxon culture.

skyclad: Naked for the purposes of worship or magical working (literally, "clad only in the sky").

Stregaria, Stregheria: An Italian tradition of witchcraft.

Summerlands: A place of rest between incarnations.

syncretism: The fusion of different beliefs, myths, concepts and/or practices from a variety of religions and/or cultures.

Thelema [θε'liːmə]: A philosophy and religion espoused in *Liber AL vel Legis* [Crowley 1904], which contains the maxim, "Do what thou wilt shall be the whole of the Law".

Traditional Initiatory Witchcraft: While taken literally this would cover any form of witchcraft in which traditions are passed down to initiates, this term is often understood to exclude post-Gardnerian Traditions, and to include only those who claim a lineage outside of that of Gardner (often claiming a longer, and hence "more traditional" lineage).

two-spirit: A modern term for Native Americans who fulfil mixed gender roles.

Yule: Derived from an Anglo-Saxon term covering two months of winter, in turn derived from the Old Norse term for a pre-Christian feast day; *Yule* came to be the name of the twelve-day feast of the Nativity of Christ, before being much replaced, though never entirely extinguished, by the name *Christmas*. Compare *Jul* in Danish, Swedish, and Norwegian. *Yule* was much revived as a term for Christmas by nineteenth century writers striving to convey a sense of "Merrie England". While still found referring to Christmas to this day, it has come to be commonly used in different strands of modern Paganism as a term for the winter solstice.

Appendix B

References

In the case of some works referenced the date of the original publication is of importance to the history explored in this work. In such cases, that date is given if it differs from the edition I consulted, and also used for the reference's label.

The nature of web references makes the year of publication sometimes difficult to determine, though best efforts for accuracy were made in each case. All web references were current as of September 2009, unless stated otherwise.

Adler, Margot. 1997. *Drawing Down the Moon: Witches, Druids, Goddess-worshippers, and Other Pagans in America Today*. London: Penguin. ISBN 014019536X.

Alder Stand Coven. 2004. "Fraud Alert!"
www.alderstand.net/fraudalert01.htm

Andreanna. 1999. "Wiccan Tools—Andreanna's Garden."
www.geocities.com/Athens/Troy/1929/tools.html
(defunct; archived copy at web.archive.org/web/20031223173301/
http://www.geocities.com/Athens/Troy/1929/tools.html).

Anonymous. 2004. "The Mi'nerwen Tradition."
www.witchvox.com/trads/trad_minerwen.html

Armstrong, Karen. 2006. *A Short History of Myth*. Edinburgh: Canongate. ISBN 184195800X.

ATC (= Aquarian Tabernacle Church). "Branches of the Pagan Tree | Aquarian Tabernacle Church."
www.aquariantabernaclechurch.org/branches-of-the-pagan-tree

References

Baxandall, Rosalyn & Gordon, Linda. 2001. *Dear Sisters: Dispatches From The Women's Liberation Movement*. New York: Basic Books. ISBN 046501707X.

Bede. 725. *De Temporum Ratione*. Monkwearmouth.

Bede. 1999. *The Reckoning of Time*. Translated by Faith Wallis. Liverpool: Liverpool University Press. ISBN 0853236933.

Bender, Hy. 2000. *The "Sandman" Companion*. London: Titan Books. ISBN 1840231645.

Bonewits, Isaac. 1979. "Defining Paganism: Paleo-, Meso-, and Neo-" www.neopagan.net/PaganDefs.html

Box Office Mojo. "The Craft (1996)." www.boxofficemojo.com/movies/?id=craft.htm

Brewer, Ebenezer Cobham. 1899. "Colcannon." *Brewer's Dictionary of Phrase and Fable*. www.bartleby.com/81/3832.html

Brown, Dan. 2003a. *The Da Vinci Code*. New York: Doubleday. ISBN 0385504209.

Brown, Michael F. 2003b. *Who Owns Native Culture?* Cambridge MA: Harvard University Press. ISBN 0674016335.

Buckland, Raymond. 1974. *The Tree—The Complete Book of Saxon Witchcraft*. Newburyport: Weiser Books. ISBN 0877282587.

Buckland, Raymond. 2002. *Buckland's Complete Book of Witchcraft*. St. Paul: Llewellyn Worldwide. ISBN 0875420508. First published 1986.

Budapest, Zsuzsanna. 1976, 2007. *The Holy Book of Women's Mysteries*. Newburyport: Weiser Books. ISBN 157863413X. First published as *The Feminist Book of Lights and Shadows*, 1976.

Burge, Constance M (creator). 1998. *Charmed* (Television). Los Angeles: The WB Television Network.

Cabot, Laurie with Cowan, Tom. 1992. *Power of the Witch: A Witch's Guide to her Craft*. New York: Penguin Arkana. ISBN 0140193685.

Calhoun, Craig J. 1994. *Social Theory and the Politics of Identity*. Oxford: Blackwell Publishing. ISBN 155786473X.

Camaralzman, KaliTime. 2002. "Converting to Paganism." www.witchvox.com/va/dt_va.html?id=4027

Cantrell, Gary. 2001. *Wiccan Beliefs & Practices*. St. Paul: Llewellyn Worldwide. ISBN 1567181120.

Cavendish, Richard. 1967. *The Black Arts*. London: Perigee. ISBN 0399500359.

CAW (= Council of American Witches). 1974. "Principles of the Wiccan Belief."

Charge = "The Charge of the Goddess." From Wiccan liturgy. For attribution of this wording to Doreen Valiente see [Farrar & Farrar 1984]. For a text which has been argued as an important influence see [Leland 1899].

Chat. 2008. "I cast a SPELL to get rid of my old man." CHAT. 26th January 2008.

Chick, Jack. 2000. "Bewitched."
www.chick.com/reading/tracts/0045/0045_01.asp

Clair, René (director). 1942. *I Married a Witch* (Motion Picture). Rene Clair Productions.

Clifton, Chas S. 1998. "Nature Religion for Real." *GNOSIS*. № 48
www.chasclifton.com/papers/forreal.html

Cochrane, Robert (AKA Bowers, Roy). 1964. "The Craft Today." *Pentagram*. Issue 2, November 1964.
www.cyberwitch.com/1734/today.htm

Cochrane, Robert. 1966a. Letter to Joe Wilson, dated 12th Night, 1966.
www.cyberwitch.com/1734/letter02.htm

Cochrane, Robert. 1966b. Letter to Joe Wilson, dated 8th April, 1966.
www.cyberwitch.com/1734/letter06.htm

COG (= Covenant of the Goddess). 1995. "Interview with Pat Devlin."
www.cog.org/nextgen/thecraft.html

Collins J A, Feeny D & Gunby J. 1997. "The cost of infertility diagnosis and treatment in Canada in 1995." *Human Reproduction*. Oxford: Oxford University Press.
humrep.oxfordjournals.org/cgi/content/abstract/12/5/951

Columbus, Chris (director). 2001. *Harry Potter and the Sorcerer's Stone* (Motion Picture). Los Angeles: 1492 Pictures.

Conway, D. J. 1990a. *Celtic Magic.* St. Paul: Llewellyn Worldwide. ISBN 0875421369.

Conway, D. J. 1990b. *Norse Magic.* St. Paul: Llewellyn Worldwide. ISBN 0875421377.

Conway, D. J. 2001. *Wicca: The Complete Craft.* Trumansburg: Crossing Press. ISBN 1580910920.

Crowley, Aleister. 1904. *Liber AL vel Legis, sub figura CCXX, as delivered by XCIII=418 to DCLXVI.* Republished in Crowley 1989a.

Crowley, Aleister. 1909. *Liber 777 vel Prolegoma Symbolica Ad Systemam Sceptico-Mysticæ Viæ Explicande, Fundamentum Hieroglyphicum Sanctissimorum Scientiæ Summæ.* First published anonymously 1909, later in Crowley, Aleister. 1977. *777 and other Qabalistic Writings of Aleister Crowley.* York Beach: Samuel Weiser. ISBN 0877282226.

Crowley, Aleister. 1989a. *The Holy Books of Thelema.* Newburyport: Weisner Books. ISBN 0877286868.

Crowley, Aleister. Desti, Mary. 1912. *Magick, Liber ABA, Book Four: Part II; Magick (Elemental Theory).* In Crowley, Aleister et al. 1998. *Magick, Liber ABA, Book Four.* York Beach: Samuel Weisner Books. ISBN 0877289190.

Crowley, Vivianne. 1989b. *Wicca: The Old Religion in the New Age.* Shaftesbury: Element Books Ltd. ISBN 0722532717

Cunningham, Scott. 1988a, 1998. *Wicca: A Guide for the Solitary Practitioner.* St. Paul: Llewellyn Worldwide. ISBN 0875421180. First published 1988.

Cunningham, Scott. 1988b. *The Truth About Witchcraft Today.* St. Paul: Llewellyn Worldwide. ISBN 087542127X.

Daly, Mary with Caputi, Jane and Rakusin, Sudie. 1987. *Websters' First New Intergalactic Wickedary of the English Language, Conjured in Cahoots with Jane Caputi.* Boston: Beacon Press. ISBN 0807067067.

Daly, Mary. 1978. *Gyn/Ecology: The Metaethics of Radical Feminism.* Boston: Beacon Press. ISBN 0807015105.

Damiana, Stella. 2005. *Sex Spells: The Magical Path to Erotic Bliss.* St. Paul: Llewellyn Worldwide. ISBN 0738711039.

Darwin, Charles. 1871. *The Descent of Man, and Selection in Relation to Sex.* London: John Murray.

Demarco, Stacey. 2006. *Witch in the Bedroom: Proven Sensual Magic.* St. Paul: Llewellyn Worldwide. ISBN 0738708445.

dragonmoondesigns. 1996. *Witchy Crafts.* www.thehealinghealers.com/creative/crafts_toc.html (defunct; archived copy at web.archive.org/web/20071221044204/http://www.thehealinghealers.com/creative/crafts_toc.html).

Drew, A. J. 2002. *Wicca for Couples, Making Magick Together.* Franklin Lakes: New Page Books. ISBN 1564146200.

Druidschool 2006. "The Three Samhains." www.druidschool.com/site/1030100/page/587337

Druidschool. 2005. "Tara na Rí." www.druidschool.com/site/1030100/page/471039

Dworkin, Andrea. 1991. *Woman Hating.* New York: Plume. ISBN 0452268273. First published Dutton, New York, 1974.

Engels, Frederich. 1884. *The Origin of the Family, Private Property, and the State: in the light of the researches of Lewis H. Morgan.*

Espenson, Jane. 1999. "Pangs" [Television Series Episode]. In Whedon 1997.

Espenson, Jane. 2000. "Superstar" [Television Series Episode]. In Whedon 1997.

Farrar, Janet & Farrar, Stewart. 1981. *Eight Sabbats for Witches.* London: Robert Hale. ISBN 0709185790. Republished in Farrar & Farrar 1996.

Farrar, Janet & Farrar, Stewart. 1984. *The Witches' Way.* Blaine: Phoenix Publishing. ISBN 0919345719. Republished in Farrar & Farrar 1996.

Farrar, Janet & Farrar, Stewart. 1996. *A Witches' Bible.* Blaine: Phoenix Publishing. ISBN 0919345921.

Farrar, Stewart. 1971, 1983. *What Witches Do.* Blaine: Phoenix Publishing. ISBN 0919345174. First published as *What Witches Do: The Modern Coven Revealed,* Peter Davies, London, 1971, ISBN 0432045708.

FBI (=Federal Bureau of Investigation). 1976. Intelligence Report "Weatherman Underground, Summary. Dated 8/20/76." Released under the Freedom of Information Act.
foia.fbi.gov/weather/weath2a.pdf

Finnin, Ann. 2008. *The Forge of Tubal Cain.* Los Angeles: Pendraig Publishing. ISBN 0979616832.

Firefox, LaSara. 2006. *Sexy Witch.* St. Paul: Llewellyn Worldwide. ISBN 073870752X.

Fitch, Ed. 2002. *Grimoire of Shadows.* St. Paul: Llewellyn. ISBN 1567186599. Taken from material by the same author distributed circa 1970.

Fleming, Andrew (director). 1996. *The Craft* (Motion Picture). Culvert City: Sony Pictures.

Fortune, Dion. 1938, 2003. *The Sea Priestess.* Newburyport: Weiser Books. ISBN 1578632900. First published 1938.

Frater Barrabbas. 2007. *The Disciple's Guide to Ritual Magick: A Beginner's Introduction to the High Art.* Stafford: Megalithica Books. ISBN 1905713088.

Frazer, Sir James. 1922. *The Golden Bough* (1922 Abridgement). www.gutenberg.org/ebooks/3623

Freud, Sigmund. 1905, 1963. *Jokes and Their Relation to the Unconscious.* New York: W. W. Norton & Company. ISBN 0393001458. First published 1905.

Fury, David. 1999. "Fear, Itself" [Television Series Episode]. In Whedon 1997.

Fury, David. 2002. "Grave" [Television Series Episode]. In Whedon 1997.

Gaiman, Neil. 2001. *American Gods.* London: Headline Book Publishing. ISBN 0747274177.

Gardner, Gerald. 1949, 1999. *High Magic's Aid.* Thame: I-H-O Books. ISBN 1872189067. First Published 1949.

Gardner, Gerald. 1954, 2004. *Witchcraft Today.* New York: Citadel Press. ISBN 0806525932. First published by Rider, London, 1954.

Gardner, Gerald. 1959, 2004. *The Meaning of Witchcraft.* Newbury: Weisner Books. ISBN 1578633095. First published by Aquarian Press, 1959.

Goths (= "4 Non Goths"). 2001a. *Why Wiccans Suck.* www.whywiccanssuck.com/ (defunct; archived copy at web.archive.org/web/*/http://www.whywiccanssuck.com).

Goths (= "4 Non Goths"). 2001b. "Movies." www.whywiccanssuck.com/craft.html (defunct; archived copy at web.archive.org/web/20021013212613/ www.whywiccanssuck.com/craft.html).

Graves, Robert. 1957. *Goodbye to All That.* New York: Bantam Doubleday Dell Publishing Group. ISBN 0385093306. First published by Jonathan Cape in 1929 later revised and republished.

Graves, Robert. 1961. *The White Goddess.* London & Boston: Faber and Faber. ISBN 0571069614. First published 1948 with subsequent editions in 1952 and 1961.

Greer, Germaine. 1970, 2002. *The Female Eunuch.* New York: Farrar, Straus and Giroux. ISBN 0374527628. First published 1970.

Greer, Germaine. 1999. *The Whole Woman.* New York: Doubleday. ISBN 0385600151.

Greyschool (= Grey School of Wizardry). 2003. *Grey School of Wizardry Website.* www.greyschool.com

Grimassi, Raven. 2008. *Crafting Wiccan Traditions: Creating a Foundation for Your Spiritual Beliefs & Practices.* St. Paul: Llewellyn Worldwide. ISBN 073871108X.

Grimm, Jacob. 1888. *Teutonic Mythology.* Grimm's Teutonic Mythology Translation Project. www.northvegr.org/lore/grimmst/013_10.php

Guerra, Elizabeth. 2008. *Writer on a Broomstick.* Arcata: R J Stewart Books. ISBN 0979140277.

Hamilton, Laurel K. 1993, 2002. *Guilty Pleasures.* New York: Jove Books. ISBN 051513449X.

Hardy, Robin (director). 1973. *The Wicker Man* (Motion Picture). British Lion Film Corporation.

Hautin-Mayer, Joanna. "When is a Celt not a Celt?."
www.cyberwitch.com/wychwood/Library/
whenIsACeltNotACelt.htm

Heselton, Philip. 2000. *Wiccan Roots: Gerald Gardner and the Modern Witchcraft Revival.* Milverton: Capall Bann Publishing. ISBN 1861631103.

Heselton, Philip. 2003. *Gerald Gardner and the Cauldron of Inspiration: An Investigation Into the Sources of Gardnerian Witchcraft.* Milverton: Capall Bann Publishing. ISBN 1861631642.

Higgie, Jennifer. 2007. *The Artists Joke* (Documents of Contemporary Art). Cambridge MA: The MIT Press. ISBN 0262582740.

Horne, Fiona. 2002. *Magickal Sex: A Witches' Guide to Beds, Knobs and Broomsticks.* London: Thorsons. ISBN 0007141335.

Horne, Fiona. 2006. *Bewitch a Man: How to Find Him and Keep Him Under Your Spell.* New York: Simon Spotlight Entertainment. ISBN 1416914749.

Hutton, Ronald. 1999. *The Triumph of the Moon: A History of Modern Pagan Witchcraft.* Oxford: Oxford University Press. ISBN 0192854496.

Hutton, Ronald. 2003. *Witches, Druids and King Arthur.* London: Hambledon & London. ISBN 1852853972.

Hutton, Ronald. 2007. *The Druids: A History.* London: Hambledon Continuum. ISBN 1852855339.

Jeralds, Scott (director). 2003. *Scooby-Doo and the Legend of the Vampire* (Motion Picture). Los Angeles: Hanna-Barbera Productions.

Johnson, Myke. 1995. "Wanting to be Indian: When Spiritual Searching turns into Cultural Theft."
www.a2u2.org/pictures/pdfs/Wabanaki%20article.pdf

K, Amber. 1998. *Covencraft: Witchcraft for Three or More.* St. Paul: Llewellyn Worldwide. ISBN 1567180183.

Karon, Paul. 1999. "Witch Hunt" [Television Series Episode]. In Tinker, John (creator). D'Elia, Bill (creator). Brenneman, Amy (creator). Tavel & Connie (creator). *Judging Amy* (Television). 1999.

Los Angeles: Barbara Hall/Joseph Stern Productions, CBS Television, 20th Century Fox.

Kauffman, L A. 1990. "The Anti-Politics of Identity." *Socialist Review*. Vol 20. Issue 1 Oakland.

Kelly, Aidan A. 1994. *Notes on Gardnerian History, 1963–1990*. Los Angeles: Art Magickal Publications. As quoted at www.oldways.org/paganway.htm

Kennedy, Senator John F. 1960. "Address to the Greater Houston Ministerial Association." Audio published at jfklibrary.org/jfkl/asset_tree/AudioVisual/Topic%20Guides/ Campaign%201960/jfk_houston_ministers_high.mp3 Transcript published at jfklibrary.org/Historical+Resources/ Archives/Reference+Desk/Speeches/JFK/JFK+Pre-Pres/1960/ Address+of+Senator+John+F. +Kennedy+to+the+Greater+Houston+Ministerial+Association.htm

Kestra. 2005. "To Bash a Fluffy Author" www.nonfluffy.com/archives/001512.html

Klein, Naomi. 2001. *No Logo*. London: Flamingo. ISBN 0312421435.

Knight, Sirona. 2002. *Faery Magick: Spells, Potions and Lore from the Earth Spirits*. Franklin Lakes: New Page Books. ISBN 1564145956.

Kolbe, Winrich, (director). 1984. "Halloween Knight" [Television Series Episode]. In Larson, Glen A. (creator). *Knight Rider* (Television). 1982. Los Angeles: Glen A. Larsons Productions.

Kretchmer, John T (director). 1998. "Something Wicca This Way Comes" [Television Series Episode]. In Burge 1998.

Kruger, Justin & Dunning, David. 1999. "Unskilled and Unaware of It: How Difficulties in Recognizing One's Own Incompetence Lead to Inflated Self-Assessments." *Journal of Personality and Social Psychology*. Vol 77. № 6. Washington, DC: American Psychological Association, Inc. www.apa.org/journals/features/psp7761121.pdf

Lady Anne. 2007. "Pilgrim Ship List by Date." www.packrat-pro.com/ships/shiplist.htm

Lady Sheba. 1971, 2002. *The Book of Shadows. St. Paul: Llewellyn Worldwide.* ISBN 0875420753. First published by Llewellyn Worldwide, 1971.

Lamond, Frederic. 2005. *Fifty Years of Wicca.* Sutton Mallet: Green Magic. ISBN 0954723015.

Landstreet, Lynna. "Why I Don't Like Scott Cunningham." www.wildideas.net/temple/library/letters/cunningham1.html

Leahy, Stephen. 2006. "POPULATION: Global Food Supply Near the Breaking Point." New York: Inter Press Service.

Leland, Charles Godfrey. 1891. *Gypsy Sorcery and Fortune Telling— Illustrated by Incantations, Specimens of Medical Magic, Anecdotes, Tales.* London: T. Fisher Unwin. www.sacred-texts.com/pag/gsft

Leland, Charles Godfrey. 1899. *Aradia, or the Gospel of the Witches.* London: David Nutt. www.sacred-texts.com/pag/aradia

Lipp, Deborah. 2007. *The Study of Witchcraft, A Guidebook to Advanced Wicca.* Newburyport: Weiser Books. ISBN 1578634091.

Lugones, María, with Rosezelle, Pat Alake. 1995. "Sisterhood and Friendship as Feminist Models." Weiss, Penny A and Friedman, Marily. *Feminism and Community.* Philadelphia: Temple University Press. ISBN 1566392772.

Manners, Kim (director). 1995. "Die Hand die Verletzt" [Television Series Episode]. In Carter, Chris (creator). *The X-Files* (Television). 1993. Los Angeles: 20th Century Fox.

Martello, Leo. 1972a or 1973. *Wica Newsletter.* № 18. As quoted in Drew 2002.

Martello, Leo. 1972b. *Black Magic, Satanism, Voodoo.* New York: HC Publishers.

McCoy, Edain. 1993. *Witta: An Irish Pagan Tradition.* St. Paul: Llewellyn Worldwide. ISBN 0875427324.

McCoy, Edain. 1996. *Lady of the Night.* St. Pauls: Llewellyn Worldwide. ISBN 1567186602.

McCoy, Edain. 2003. *The Witches Coven*. St. Paul: Llewellyn Worldwide. ISBN 0738703885.

Miller, George (director). 1987. *The Witches of Eastwick* (Motion Picture). Los Angeles: Warner Brothers Pictures.

Minoan (= The Minoan Brotherhood). "Frequently Asked Questions." www.minoan-brotherhood.org

Mitchell, Karen. 2005. "Moving Beyond Wicca 101." www.suite101.com/article.cfm/wicca_witchcraft/113995

Moore, Christy (Singer). 2005. *The Burning Times* (Music Album). Sony International.

Morgan, Robin. 1970. "Goodbye to All That." New York: *Rat Subterranean News*. January 1970. blog.fair-use.org/2007/09/29/goodbye-to-all-that-by-robin-morgan-1970

Morgan, Robin. 1994. *The Word of a Woman: Feminist Dispatches, 1968–1992*. New York: W W Norton & Co Inc. ISBN 0393034275.

Morgan, Robin. 2008. "Goodbye To All That (#2)." www.womensmediacenter.com/ex/020108.html

Murphy-Hiscock, Arin. 2005. *Solitary Wicca for Life: A Complete Guide to Mastering the Craft on Your Own*. Massachusetts: Provenance Press. ISBN 1593373538.

Nobel Beyer, Catherine. 2002. *Wicca: For the Rest of Us*. wicca.timerift.net

Nobel Beyer, Catherine. 2006a. "Why We Despise Silver Ravenwolf." wicca.timerift.net/ravenwolf.shtml

Nobel Beyer, Catherine. 2006b. "Books to Avoid." wicca.timerift.net/books_avoid.shtml

Nobel Beyer, Catherine. 2006c. "Questions to the Author, Archive Two." wicca.timerift.net/letters2.shtml

Nock, Judy Ann. 2005. *A Witch's Grimoire: Create Your Own Book of Shadows*. Avon, Massachusetts: Provenance Press. ISBN 1593374070.

NWC (= New Wiccan Church). 2004. *NWC Article: British Traditional Wicca FAQ*. www.newwiccanchurch.net/articles/btwfaq.htm

(defunct; archived copy at web.archive.org/web/20080206061229/
http://www.newwiccanchurch.net/articles/btwfaq.htm).

O'Brien, Lora. 2004. *Irish Witchcraft from an Irish Witch.* Franklin Lakes:
New Page Books. ISBN 1564147592.

O'Connor, Sinéad. 1994. *Universal Mother* (Music Album). Milwaukee:
Ensign.

Oates, Joyce Carol (ed.). 1992. *The Oxford Book of American Short Stories.*
Oxford: Oxford University Press. ISBN 0195070658.

OED (= Oxford Dictionaries). 2005. *Compact Oxford English Dictionary of
Current English.* Oxford: Oxford University Press. ISBN 019861022X.

Payne, Roz. 2000. "WITCH, the rest of the story." Post to "sixties-l"
mailing list by one of the authors of a chant used against the House
Unamerican Activities Committee.
dmmc.lib.virginia.edu/lists_archive/sixties-l/2251.html

Peck, Michael Scott. 2002. *The Road Less Traveled: A New Psychology of Love,
Traditional Values, and Spiritual Growth.* New York: Simon & Schuster.
ISBN 0743238257

Pennethorne Hughes, James. 1952. *Witchcraft.* London: Longmans,
Green & Co. Ltd. ISBN 0750937246.

"Peregrine". 2007. "dot_pagan_snark: More of an 'overheard', but still
snarkworthy."
community.livejournal.com/dot_pagan_snark/416720.html

Perseus, Enyo. 2001. "Diluting Wicca"
www.wargoddess.net/essay/dilutingwicca.php

Peters, R S. 1969. *The Concept of Education.* London: Routledge & Kegan
Paul. ISBN 0710062699.

Piercy, Marge. 1972, 1995. *Eight Chambers of the Heart: Selected Poems.*
London: Penguin Books Ltd. ISBN 0140236376.

Pirsig, Robert M. 1974. *Zen and the Art of Motorcycle Maintenance: An Inquiry
Into Values.* Morrow. ISBN 0688002307.

Plath, Slyvia. 1965, 1968. *Ariel.* London: Faber & Faber. ISBN
0571086268. First published UK 1965 and US 1966.

Plath, Slyvia. 2002. *Collected Poems.* London: Faber & Faber. ISBN 0571118380.

Plath, Slyvia. Hughes, Ted (ed.). 1998. *The Journals of Sylvia Plath.* New York: Anchor Books. ISBN 0385493916.

Pliny the Elder. Bostock, John (ed.), Riley, H. T. (ed.). 1855. *The Natural History.* London: Taylor and Francis.
www.perseus.tufts.edu/cgi-bin/ptext?lookup=Plin.+Nat.+toc

Pratchett, Terry. 1992. *Lords and Ladies.* London: Victor Gollancz Ltd. ISBN 0575052236.

Quine, Richard (director). 1958. *Bell Book and Candle* (Motion Picture). Julian Blaustine Productions Ltd.

Ravenwolf, Silver. 1993. *To Ride a Silver Broomstick.* St. Paul: Llewellyn Worldwide. ISBN 087542791X.

Ravenwolf, Silver. 1998. *Teen Witch: Wicca for a New Generation.* St. Paul: Llewellyn Worldwide. ISBN 1567187250.

Ravenwolf, Silver. 1999. *To Stir a Magick Cauldron: A Witch's Guide to Casting and Conjuring.* St. Paul: Llewellyn Worldwide. ISBN 1567184243.

Raymond, Eric S. 2001. "Homesteading the Noosphere." *The Cathedral and the Bazaar.* Sebastopol: O'Reilly and Associates. ISBN 0596001088.

Red Road Collective. 1993. *Red Road Collective Newsletter.* Spring 1993.
www.geocities.com/redroadcollective/NewsletterS93.html

Renshaw, Jeannine. 2000. "I've Got You Under My Skin" [Television series episode]. In Whedon, Josh (Creator) & Greenwalt, David (Creator). *Angel* (television), 2000. Los Angeles: Mutant Enemy & 20th Century Fox.

Renshaw, Jeannine. 2007. "Mean Ghost" [Television series episode] in Gray, John (Creator), *Ghost Whisperer* (television), Los Angeles: ABC Studios, Burbank.

Robinson, B A. 1996–2008. "Glossary of religious terms starting with the letter 'B'." www.religioustolerance.org/gl_b.htm

Roninwolf. 2008. "No Standardization Without Representation."

References

www.witchvox.com/va/dt_va.html?a=usny&c=words&id=12802

Rowan, John. 1987. *The Horned God: Feminism and Men as Wounding and Healing*. London: Routledge. ISBN 041504524X.

Rowling, J. K. 1997. *Harry Potter and the Philosopher's Stone*. London: Bloomsbury Publishing. ISBN 0747532745. Published in the US as *Harry Potter and the Sorcerer's Stone*, 1998.

Saille, Harmonia. 2006. "Fluffy Bunny."
www.witchdom.com/index.php?option=com_content&id=29

Saks, Sol (creator). 1964–1972. *Bewitched* (Television). Los Angeles: Screen Gems.

Sanders, Alex, et al. 1984. *The Alex Sanders Lectures*. New York: Magickal Childe Inc. ISBN 0939708051.

Schlüter, Hans Holmskov. 2007. "Danish Resistance during the Holocaust."
www.holocaustresearchproject.org/revolt/danishresistance.html

Scovell, Nell (creator). 1996. *Sabrina the Teenage Witch* (Television). Los Angeles: Heartbreak Films.

Shakespeare, William, 1623. *Mr. William Shakespeares Comedies, Histories, & Tragedies*. London: Issac Jaggard & Edward Blount.

Silverlotus. 2004-2006. *Wicca and Witchcraft: The Differences*.
lotuspond.silentblue.net/wicca/wiccadifferences.html

Starhawk. 1979, 1989. *Spiral Dance: A Rebirth of the Ancient Religion of the Great Goddess*. San Francisco: Harper. ISBN 0062508148.

Stepanich, Kisma K. 1994. *Faery Wicca, Book 1: Theory and Magick, a Book of Shadows and Lights*. St. Paul: Llewellyn Worldwide. ISBN 1567186947.

Stepanich, Kisma K. 1998. *Faery Wicca, Book 2: The Shamanic Practices of the Cunning Arts*. St. Paul: Llewellyn Worldwide. ISBN 1567186955.

Strenstrum, Jim (director). 1999. *Scooby-Doo and the Witches Ghost* (Motion Picture). Los Angeles: Hanna-Barbera Productions.

Sutton, Maya Magee & Mann, Nicholas R. 2000. *Druid Magic: The Practice of Celtic Wisdom*. St. Paul: Llewellyn Worldwide. ISBN 1567184812.

215

Taylor, Gordon Rattray. 1954. *Sex in History*. New York: Vanguard Press. ISBN 0814902200.

The Combahee River Collective. 1977. *Combahee River Collective Statement*. Dated April 1977. circuitous.org/scraps/combahee.html

Thompson, Lady Gwen. 1975. "The Rede of the Wiccae." www.nectw.org/ladygwynne.html First published in *Green Egg*, issue 69, 1975.

Thoreau, Henry David. 1854. *Walden; or, Life in the Woods*. Boston: Ticknor and Fields.

Tiamat. 1998. "Wicca txt." www.xs4all.nl/~tiamat/wicca.htm

Tiele, Cornelis Petrus. 1902. "Religion." *Encyclopædia Britannica*. Ninth Edition.

Twilight, Lady Riona. 2006. *The Tools of the Trade*. www.freewebs.com/lady_riona_twilight/thetoolsthatiuse.htm

Utah (= Utah State Courts). 2008. "High Profile Court Cases—State of Utah v. Warren Steed Jeffs". www.utcourts.gov/media/hpcases/index.cgi?mode=selectcategory&category_id=334

Whedon, Josh. 1997. *Buffy the Vampire Slayer* (Television). Los Angeles: Mutant Enemy & 20th Century Fox.

Whedon, Josh. 1999. "Hush." [Television series episode]. in Whedon 1997.

Whedon, Josh. 2000a. "Who are You." [Television series episode]. In Whedon 1997.

Whedon, Josh. 2000b. "Restless." [Television series episode]. In Whedon 1997.

Wikipedia. 2006. "Talk:British Traditional Wicca." en.wikipedia.org/wiki/Talk:British_Traditional_Wicca

Wikipedia. 2007. "Wikipedia: The Spiral Dance." en.wikipedia.org/w/index.php?title=The_Spiral_Dance&oldid=117031831

Witchschool (= Witch School International, Inc). 2001. *WitchSchool.com Website*. www.witchschool.com

Index

Printed in June 2019
by Rotomail Italia S.p.A., Vignate (MI) - Italy